A Rusty Needle

BY IVAN V. LALIĆ

TRANSLATED BY FRANCIS R. JONES

The Works of Love
1981

Last Quarter
1987

The Passionate Measure
1989

IVAN V. LALIĆ

A Rusty Needle

TRANSLATED BY
FRANCIS R. JONES

ANVIL PRESS POETRY

Published in 1996
by Anvil Press Poetry Ltd
69 King George Street London SE10 8PX

This book is published
with financial assistance from
The Arts Council of England

Designed and composed by Anvil
Photoset in Plantin by Typestream
Printed in England
by Morganprint (Blackheath) Ltd
Distributed by Password, Manchester

ISBN 0 85646 241 1

IN MEMORY OF VLAJKO

ACKNOWLEDGEMENTS

Thanks are given to *Comparative Criticism* for permission to reproduce the following poems: 'A Rusty Needle', 'Ophelia', 'Wind', 'Prayer', 'Byzantium', 'Bees', 'Slavery', 'The Flower of Beginning', 'Rain After Us' and 'The Sea Described from Memory'.

CONTENTS

III *Melissa: Twenty-Four Fragments*

IV

V

VI

VII   *Kalemegdan*

VIII

IX *Dubrovnik, A Winter's Tale*

X *Of the Works of Love, or Byzantium*

INTRODUCTION

Names as a Bribe to Time: The Poetry of Ivan V. Lalić

IVAN V. LALIĆ is rapidly becoming recognised as the leading living poet of what once was Yugoslavia. Born in Belgrade in 1931, he finished high school and studied law in Zagreb, where his first volumes of poetry appeared. He now lives for most of the year in Belgrade, but – at least until the civil war – he has spent every summer in Rovinj, on the northern Adriatic Coast. His wife, Branka, who is Croatian, works for Yugoslavia's international youth music organisation. In 1989 their elder son, Vlajko, was drowned in a storm while sailing from Venice to Rovinj.

Ivan V. Lalić has published the following collections of poetry:

> *Bivši dečak* (Once a Boy), 1955
> *Vetrovito proleće* (Windy Spring), 1956
> *Velika vrata mora* (The Great Gates of the Sea), 1958
> *Melisa* (Melissa), 1959
> *Argonauti i druge pesme* (The Argonauts and Other
>   Poems), 1961
> *Vreme, vatre, vrtovi* (Time, Fires, Gardens), 1961
> *Čin* (Act), 1963
> *Krug* (Circle), 1968
> *Izabrane i nove pesme* (Collected and New Poems), 1969
> *Smetnje na vezama* (Fading Contact), 1975
> *Strasna mera* (The Passionate Measure), 1984
> *Pesme* (Poems), 1987
> *Vizantija* (Byzantium), 1988
> *Pismo* (Script), 1992

Until his recent retirement, Lalić was a senior editor at the Nolit publishing house. He is also well-known as writer of literary criticism, and as a translator of poetry – he has translated Whitman, Eliot and Hölderlin into Serbo-Croat, and has published anthologies of modern French and American poetry (the latter in collaboration with Branka Lalić).

Ivan V. Lalić's own works have gained many national and international awards, and have been translated into many languages. In the British Isles, two editions of his verse have appeared,

13

both with the present translator: a selection entitled *The Works of Love* (Anvil, 1981), and an integral translation of *The Passionate Measure* (Anvil, with Dedalus of Dublin, 1989), which gained the 1991 European Poetry Translation Prize. In the United States, two selections of his poems have appeared in Charles Simic's translation: *Fire Gardens* (New Rivers Press, 1970) and *Roll Call of Mirrors* (Wesleyan University Press, 1989).

The present work – which I have retitled *A Rusty Needle* after the first, key poem – is a virtually complete version (all but two poems) of the *Izabrane i nove pesme* of 1969. It is a work of vital importance to the reader of Lalić's poetry – for two reasons. Firstly, Lalić's early books have long been out of print: in this volume, however, he assembled what he still regards as the definitive selection of his early verse. Then, to this important retrospective he added the magnificent Dubrovnik and Byzantium cycles, which pay homage to his country's Eastern and Western heritages in turn. In their sheer scope, in their unity, depth and beauty of vision, these two great poetic pilgrimages are among his most impressive poetic achievements to date.

Thus *A Rusty Needle* traces Lalić's artistic development from his first published poems in his early twenties to the onset of his mature period. Here three, perhaps four, overlapping phases can be seen. The clear-cut poems of his youth, painting the events and moods of personal past or myth. The dense, colourful, highly-charged imagery of a middle period, which reached its height in the 'Melissa' poems of 1959. Finally, the great philosophical explorations of history and myth, whose scalpel-sharp images cut to the core of experience, revealing the layers of universal meaning beneath the skin of events. But woven through this, a strand which is to determine works to come: the same breathtaking sharpness of imagery in the service of the same quest for universality, but with the poet's experience of the here and now as its theme – love, childbirth, landscape ... – a realisation that the everyday can also become lucidly, radiantly charged with a universal vision.

Though the verse of Ivan V. Lalić may vary in style and theme, it has one constant quality: an intense joy in the visual. He paints a whole world for us to explore, a world which is recognisable as our own, but one with a richer, intenser resonance. Elemental images – sun, wind, rain, sea – are interspersed with sophisticated yet vividly sensual metaphors. A movement opens a summer dress 'as light opens a flower'; late frost is on the peach blossom 'like salt on a wound'. Simple joy in the here and now – the happiness of love, the beauty of the sensory world:

> a lake polished
> Like marble, ornate with veins of light,
> A clearing heaped with ozone between two rains,
> A safe afternoon, shingled roofs
> Rinsed and dried to the patina of old silver . . .

['Algol', 3]

merges, without a boundary, with complex philosophical musings on life, time, memory and the poet's art.

In his poetic world, as lucid as crystal, so intensely *seen*, opaque barriers turn transparent – the barriers that separate, in our world, closeness from distance, the instant from history, the living from the dead, the self from the other, the real from the ideal, experience from the words that preserve it.

A crucial barrier is that between dead and living, past and present. Once, at the beginning of a BBC interview, Lalić was asked how he had found his poetic voice. Picking up a copy of *Izabrane i nove pesme* from the table, he said: 'My first book had the title *Once a Boy*. My childhood and boyhood in the war marked very strongly everything I ever wrote as a poem or poetry. In this book, the first poem, "A Rusty Needle", is a poem about my school-friends, who were my age and perished in an air raid . . . and I remained to remember . . . The theme of death in my poetry, or destruction, is very deeply rooted in this war experience.'

In revealing a childhood trauma as the key to his poetic oeuvre, Lalić reminds us that his concern with transience – the beauty and fragility of the present instant, and memory, its sole and flawed preservation – is rooted in personal experience. This is why the early poems which tell of the happiness of childhood and his brutal coming of age – the slaughter of his friends in the air raid when he was ten, the death of his mother two years later – are crucial to an understanding of his whole work, where the abstract and metaphysical are intimately mixed with the personal, the directly experienced, the intensely felt. It explains why the keywords such as misfortune, wisdom, and memory, which one meets throughout his verse, have a strange directness: forces of nature, perhaps, like wind, sea and sun, rather than abstract concepts.

15

If Lalić knows misfortune to be a condition of life, he knows a little wisdom to be its meagre, bitter fruit, all the more valued for being so dearly won; and memory to be his life's painful, unshirkable duty. This, therefore, is his poetic task:

> to grow on
> With their gaze in the nape of my neck, like
> A rusty needle just under the skin . . .
>
> ['A Rusty Needle']

Later, in the more mature third phase, Lalić explores the fragility not only of individual human beings and their physical works, but also of their accumulated wisdom and culture. These explorations are on a grand plane: the death of civilisations (Byzantium, medieval Serbia), the archetypal tragedies of myth (Orpheus, Odysseus). Obliteration is the human condition:

> Our works are bounded by emptiness,
> Their edges brittle, islands strewn across the sea;
> How much silence on every feeble word,
> How much sky on every standing column,
> How much terrible harmony in the ruins!
>
> ['Lament of the Chronicler']

Set against this fragility, there is again only memory, again only the memory of fragile individuals. Though memory may be unreliable, fragmented, dying with the rememberer, yet it can give a provisional immortality, passed down the generations as folk memory or legend. But when a civilisation is destroyed, when a race is slaughtered or scattered, when its books are burnt and its language forgotten, memory's thin thread may break. Then, even if the strands are rediscovered, by chance, centuries later, they may no longer be understood, for the pattern is missing, the reason for its weaving is forgotten:

> The guard on the shore, invisible, forgotten,
> Stares at the open green sea,
> For someone must stay, meaningless,
> If the game is to be played correctly.
>
> And the right password rusts in his mouth
> Like a key in an unneeded keyhole.
>
> ['The Guard in Colchis']

16

At one point Lalić asks: if time levels all, is there a refuge beyond time, a 'Home of the Swans' which outlives its dreamer? Perhaps there is – but if it is out of time, it is also out of space, out of our world. The ghosts who live there – like the guard in Colchis, or like the blessed in the New Jerusalem, a cold comfort for the loss of their earthly Byzantium – cannot communicate with us. For our world swiftly changes; their world, if it exists at all, is left behind in a timeless but uncomprehended past.

In the end, it is in our world, this fragile present, that we live and act. What is important is the effort to hand on the torch, against all odds. As Jason says in 'The Argonauts':

> the end does not matter,

What matters is only the sailing.

It is here that hope lies, even if the effort fails.

But if time destroys, time heals too: the scars of war are erased as effectively as the works of love. Perhaps then it is more important that love be made again and again in the present, ignorant or heedless of the past and its hard-won wisdom, its pain:

> but listen to the screams of the birds
> Over the cove where the sea learns from lovers
> A different tenderness: time is impartial,
> And the world is love's task,
> > the long rehearsal
> Of immature gods.

['Of the Works of Love']

And yet, though there be no permanence, obliteration too is rarely pure. There remain beautiful ruins, scattered signs, voices on the wind. Though the meaning of the message is lost, some communication takes place: the past infects the present, the process of accidental transmission can continue. And this is the poet's task, to help this process: to unearth the statue, to hear the voices of the ghosts in the wind. When, in the final poem of the book, the chronicler, waiting for his world to end, cries out in despair:

> And then who would wish to compose our testimony
> From these scattered syllables, from the cries
> Caught by chance in some antique mirror,
> In the surge of a wave? And why?

['Byzantium VII']

it is the poet of today who hears him, who transmits his cries, just as he speaks the voices of his childhood friends from under the rubble.

From dead to living, from past to present: these are just two of the distances Lalić attempts to bridge. Sometimes the distances may be literal, physical: the endless voyage; the quest whose aim is forgotten as the years go by; the soldier who dies in a forgotten battle in a far-off land. These archetypal images of the human journey towards a hard self-knowledge have literary and folk resonances down the ages: Homer's Odysseus, the Tang soldier poets writing home from a distant frontier, the Wandering Jew, Eliot's Journey of the Magi.

Another distance is out of time and space, but closely connected to both: the gap between the real world and the words we use to describe it. Reality is fleeting; by recording reality, the poet's words give the instant permanence, but they are a poor substitute: they can never properly convey experience itself. Nevertheless, the act of recording, memory's most powerful weapon, must be performed if experience is not to be lost. It is the poet's solemn duty to perform this task – even though, by stepping back in order to record, he may forfeit the ability to experience the moment for what it is:

> All my words, my speech,
> My knife beneath the pillow, the glass of water on the table,
> Images bartered for the right to pronounce them,
> Names I slip as a bribe to time,
> And birds I ring with the fragile silver of memory . . .
>
> ['Algol', 4]

Lalić's poetic ideal, however, is to breach the barriers separating here and now from wider experience – present from past, the deed from the word that records it, the self from the other. The fragile instant when these barriers dissolve is what we call happiness: the 'clear time' when

> Everything is already uttered, the space separating
> Word and deed, fire and rose, is repealed,
> Misfortune excluded:
> this is where I listen to you
> Tonight . . .
>
> ['Then you may have said...']

18

These instants of harmony, which he later calls 'spaces of hope', are so intense that no thought, no words are needed to give them permanence – for the moment, anyway. They may occur through love, where it is the Other who breaches the boundary of the poet's self:

> When you go, space closes over like water behind you,
> Do not look back: there is nothing outside you,
> Space is only time visible in a different way,
> Places we love we can never leave.

['Places We Love']

Or they may occur through experience of the world, when sensation is so intense that the self, the observer, becomes dissolved in the observed, and forgets the need to record:

>   as the wet, glittering voices
> Of birds in the garden opposite, already peeled bare,
> Enter through the window like bullets of gentleness;
> Still, phosphor mornings of love,
>
> As the room blossoms into a hall of mirrors
> Duplicating a single movement, or maybe the colour
> Of a dress on a chair . . .

['Roman Quartet', II]

A final distance Lalić bridges is that between cultures. As I write, Yugoslavia is savagely tearing herself apart along ancient fault-lines: it is easy now to forget the riches of her culture, a culture whose wealth was its very diversity, laying claim to the legacies of Austria-Hungary and the Ottoman Empire, Catholicism and Orthodoxy, Central Europe and the Mediterranean.

Though Lalić writes in the Serbian dialect and lives in Serbia, his formative years were shared between Zagreb and Belgrade, the Croat and Serb capitals, and he spends several months a year on the Adriatic Coast.

He pays homage to the twin sources of his pan-Yugoslav heritage in the two major historical cycles of this volume. In the Dubrovnik cycle, he travels West, on a pilgrimage to a Croatian literary shrine. It was in the Renaissance Golden Age of Dalmatia, with the city-state of Dubrovnik at its heart, that literature in the Croatian vernacular had its first great blossoming.

In the Byzantium cycle he looks East, to the roots of the Serbian culture. The medieval Serbian state, whose history Lalić celebrates in Part II of the present work, grew up under the influence of the Eastern Roman or Byzantine Empire. At one point in the fourteenth century she seemed poised to become Byzantium's successor, only to be brought down with her mentor as the Ottoman Turks tightened their grip on the Balkans. Though the best-known legacy of medieval Serbia is her magnificent frescoed monasteries, it was in this age that the first religious and secular literature was written in the Serbian dialect of Old Slavonic.

Lalić, however, would probably describe himself less as a Yugoslav than as a Mediterranean poet. There is a radiant sense of light in Lalić's poetry. The vivid Franciscan elements of fire and wind, lightning and water, sea and stars are ever present – especially the sea, a source to which he constantly returns:

> Maybe the south, that warm, violet sea,
> Riddled with windfall stars between the tree-
> Clad shores, their droves of scented pine ablaze,
> The tinder of light . . .

> [*Melissa* 14, 'South']

The imagery of water and light, the blaze of primary colours, the warm Mediterranean gentleness which pervades Lalić's poetry, reveals a closer kinship with poets such as Seferis, Montale and Valéry, than with his influential compatriots such as Vasko Popa, the mythic surrealist, or Branko Miljković, the lyricist of death (addressed in Lalić's 'Spring Liturgy for a Dead Poet').

For Lalić, however, the Mediterranean is more than a source of images, however radiant: it is a cultural concept which reaches beyond his beloved Adriatic. Here, in the Eastern Mediterranean, he sees the Judaeo-Christian fatefulness of the Near East merging with the easy animism of Ancient Greece:

> that land of gracious beasts, which raise
> Their heads, hornless and horned, to hear the singing,

> The homeland of springs which mutter words, then grow
> Opaque as fable . . .

> [*Melissa* 14, 'South']

to form the culture we call European. Seen in this light, Dubrovnik and Byzantium are not so much sources of national pride as lenses focusing the wisdom of older cultures (through Dubrovnik: Italy and Venice; through Byzantium: Ancient and Byzantine Greece) to light the tinder of South Slav culture – cultural memory in action.

Lalić also integrates Northern European influences into his poetry. The combination of easy diction with dense, charged images reminds us of Eliot, Pound and Yeats, for instance. Indeed, certain motifs, such as that of the falcon, may strike familiar chords with the English-speaking reader – compare Yeats'

> Turning and turning in the widening gyre
> The falcon cannot hear the falconer . . .

with Lalić's

> If, in the end, one has to die, it is fine
> To die with a falcon, one's own falcon,
> Circling and looking for a black bird in the blue
> Circle of sky, mad and blind with light.
>
> ['Death with a Falcon']

or, more directly:

> I shy
> At the meaning of the image as old as a dream:
> The star cannot hear the frenzied falconer's cry.
>
> [*Melissa* 3, 'Star']

No true poet quotes another, however, without adding a extra layer of significance. The falcon, for instance, is already a loaded symbol for Yugoslavs – in the folk epic, it signifies the lone hero. Anyway, we should not arrogantly assume that similarity of themes means that they must have been borrowed. For example, in conversations with English-speaking readers Lalić often has to stress that Yeats's Byzantium had no influence on his own: 'Yeats's Byzantium is looked from the outside, but mine is from the inside: that is why they are so different.'

Affinity with other Northern European poetries may also be detected. Lalić has a great love for Hölderlin, Europe's first modernist poet – see, for instance, the opening quote of 'Requiem for a Mother'. Shakespeare's Ophelia is the overt theme of another early poem; a closer reading, however, reveals it to be perhaps more of an homage to Rimbaud's 'Le Bâteau Ivre' – the endless, phantasmagoric voyage of a deserted, drifting boat – than to Shakespeare:

21

Slow your progress: bridges quiver,
Sails are bathed in the heat of the sun.
Death in your flesh, the gurgling river
Beneath you: is your suffering done?

['Ophelia']

A seam which Lalić mines surprisingly little (in contrast with Vasko
Popa, say) is his country's folk poetry, which provided the main
grounding for the establishment of literary Serbo-Croat in the
nineteenth century, and which has strongly influenced poetry –
especially in Serbia – ever since. Where Lalić does use folk motifs,
his aim is usually to underline a 'folk' theme, such as in 'The Dark
Province' (see the notes for the folk tale underlying this poem). Or
in 'Princip on the Battlefield', where Lalić draws deliberate parallels
between the Sarajevo assassination of 1914 and the cataclysmic
Battle of Kosovo, feted in many a heroic ballad, on the same day
525 years before (see the notes for details). Or in 'Smederevo':

Our Lord the Prince
Drinks wine as golden as the carp in the river . . .

– a typical folk-epic formula.

Paradoxically, however, it is in his very assimilation of influ-
ences from North and South, East and West, rather than in a
faithfulness to folk roots, that Lalić shows himself to be a truly
Yugoslav poet. For it was in this merging of diverse influences that
the vibrancy of Yugoslav literary, artistic and popular culture lay. It
is this culture's deliberate destruction from within (the most, per-
haps the only, effective way to destroy a culture) that is post-war
Europe's greatest tragedy.

*   *   *

In terms of poetic form, Lalić is his country's acknowledged master
craftsman. Though the majority of the poems in this collection are
in blank verse, many are written in more tightly-structured forms.
Interestingly, it is here, rather than in subject matter or diction,
that his roots in national tradition can be more clearly discerned.

Traditional South Slav verse tends not to be rhymed, but has
strict rules in terms of line-length. These rules, however, are rather
different from those of English metrics. English is a 'stress-timed'

language: in speech as in poetry, the underlying beat tends to be set by the stressed syllables, with unstressed syllables squeezing in between – none, one, two or even three at a time – as best they can:

All in the | *val*ley of | *death* | *rode* the six | *hun*dred

Serbo-Croat, however, like French, Italian and many other languages, is 'syllable-timed': in other words, the underlying beat of the language is set by the syllables themselves – the difference can be heard most strongly in rapid speech, where we think that foreigners jabber, but they accuse of us of swallowing our words! Thus the traditional South Slav poetic line is defined in terms of how many syllables it contains: the *narodni deseterac* ('folk ten-syllable'), for instance, and especially the eleven-syllable *jedanaesterac*, are used in several of Lalić's poems. Part 1 of 'Spring Liturgy for a Dead Poet', for example, opens with a *deseterac*, but then continues in the *jedanaesterac*:

> *Jesi li sada sam? Dovoljno sam*
> *Da kažeš zemlji: evo novo ime*
> *Za sećanje, za ukus, za tvoj očaj*
> *U proleće kad moraš biti čudo . . .*

> Are you alone at last? Alone enough
> To say to the earth: here is another name
> For memory, for taste, for the despair which
> Fills you when spring insists that you become a
> Miracle . . .

Of course, Lalić also uses 'foreign' forms besides the blank verse already mentioned. Several of his poems are also rhymed, and a few use stress-rhythms rather than syllable-counts – the 'Melissa' cycle, for instance, which is made up of irregularly-rhymed sonnets in a hexameter rhythm. Two other poems are written in Sapphics: a verse form which has strict rules in terms of both syllable and stress counts (three lines ' . | ' . | ' . . | ' . | ' . plus one line ' . . | ' .):

> *Najzad opet poznajem ovaj blesak,*
> *Vedru brazdu pučine, zasejanu*
> *Kratkom vatrom godina koje pamtim,*
> *Semenom smene . . .*

> Now I know this flash, once again, at last, this
> Still and limpid furrow of ocean, sown with

Short-lived fire, the years I remember, with the
Seeds of transition ...

['The Sea After Rain']

The use of rhyme and rhythm poses interesting problems for the translator. One is the sheer drudgery of trying to force a given meaning into a given structure, but in a different language. Here many translators take the easy way out, translating everything into blank verse. This tactic, which I used in *The Works of Love* (1981), I now feel gives a degradation, a flattening of the poet's original intention – especially when, as with Lalić, a wide variety of verse forms are used, ranging from blank verse to rhymed syllabic forms.

Hence I have now tried to reproduce Lalić's original structure wherever possible, even at the expense of expanding or compressing an image here and there. Thus, in the above example: 'Now' is an addition to the first line; *Vedru* – serene, clear (sky), fair (weather) – has been expanded to 'Still and limpid'; and *koje* – which – has been deleted from 'the years I remember'. On the other hand, because every word in Serbo-Croat has a grammatical ending, a given phrase tends to have more syllables than its English equivalent. Thus, rather than pad out every line in a poem, I have sometimes compressed the metre – writing many of the 'Melissa' poems as pentameters rather than hexameters, for instance:

Prastaro jutro, kad sva su lica bogova slična,
U jetkom praskozorju, svirepa, nepomična,
Jednako mokra od tudjih suza, zelena od plesni,
U osmehu što otkriva naoružane desni ...

An age-old morning: the gods all show the same
Face in the caustic daybreak, immobile and cold,
All wet with others' tears, all green with mould,
Their smiles revealing beweaponed gums; no aim ...

[*Melissa* 20, 'Morning']

Another reason for choosing a pentameter solution was that this is a popular poetic line in English; hexameters are much less common, and are often accused of having a rather heavy, overloaded feel to the English-speaking reader.

The original poet may even use forms which simply do not exist in the target language. English poetry, for example, does not use purely syllabic lines. This is no reason to avoid them in translation; but if they are used, there is a double risk. On the one hand, the English-speaking reader will almost certainly not recognise them as syllabic. On the other hand, a vague sensation of regularity without stress-rhythm will give the irritating impression that 'this poem doesn't scan'. For this reason I have taken a belt-and-braces approach: I use syllabic lines in the translation where appropriate, but I have tried (admittedly, not always with success) to add a regular rhythm as an overlay, as in the 4-beat by 8-syllable line:

> The compass needle spins around
> In frantic search for signs unfound,
> In death's own field her songs resound.

['A Bitter Summer's Fires Still Wheel']

There are other areas than rhyme and rhythm, of course, where Ivan V. Lalić shows his mastery of the craft of poetry. His stunning use of metaphor and simile have already been mentioned. No less stunning is his choice of the exact word or phrase, ranging skilfully from the complex and subtle to the direct and elemental, depending on the mood he wishes to convey:

>   we translated
> An unknown tongue into known forms,
> And celebrated that unspoken agreement
> With the stronger measure of substance;
>
> Then the earth shook –
>
> Somewhere there had been a mistake,
>
>   unclear even in the flash
> Of dust settling, of the tongue melting
> Into its genesis, like water;
> When the blood was dry
> We tried again.

['The Masons']

Moreover, these words are linked into structures of sound by means of rhythmic patterning, alliteration and vowel rhyme – which I have tried to reproduce wherever possible (a far easier task than finding rhymes!). Though prominent, this sound-patterning is never over-done . . . except for a line and a half of marvellous self-parody:

Grubi greben, grad grohota grobova,
Groktanje grba . . .

Scarred scarp, skyline of scoffing scaffolds, screeching
Escutcheons . . .

['Chamber Poem for a City']

The reader of Serbo-Croat may spot the fact that I have not been
scrupulously literal in my version, but you can't win them all . . . In
any case, what makes poetry reach beyond prose – and what makes
Lalić's poetry so dazzling – is its joyful recognition that there is
more to words than meaning alone.

FRANCIS R. JONES
Ovingham, Northumberland
1993

I

A RUSTY NEEDLE

Then I came to love the night, to love it for the wind teased
Through the dark needles of the pines, and the rapping of the
Shutter at the window of the solid house, whose foundations
Are all that remain, and the green rust of weeds.

When the wind was gone, the crickets remained,
And my mother's breath, rightwards in the dark,
Tepid and gentle. I sank into sleep as if into soapy water,
Quickly, softly, without a ripple upon the surface.

Summers on the mountain's shoulder, between the cones;
In the wind, beneath my dark skin, the small bones
Grew. Guests would come to the green-eyed house,
Though I was forever all grubby with resin.

Autumn – that was the city. The gentle fall of a street
Spanned with the triumphal arch of children's laughter.
Little moves in the shadow of a big world
Beginning to shake on its feet of clay.

Oh, there were so many of us. Each a meek cadet
Of a green life that loved us all alike.
Castaways and citizens all, cocooned as yet,
Harts and roughnecks, squid-soft still.

But we were caught in a net, like a salty sea-crop
Shimmering, viscid, through chilly depths.
I lived to see a summer in a wounded city,
My mouth full of fear like ground glass.

Then I came to hate the night, to hate it for the fear
Teased through the echo of footsteps in the street.
For a full-grown childhood plucked to the blood,
And the feathers flying at a knife of black breath.

I picture the ones born with me, the ones
Now deep in their deaths. Each a meek cadet

Of a green life, who outgrew me by a death,
All of a sudden, against their will.

Did they really come of age in an instant, just
Before they crumpled like poppies under the scree
Of rubble, their eyes full of fear and dust,
Dumbstruck, for this was not what they wanted?

I don't know. But I remained, to grow on
With their gaze in the nape of my neck, like
A rusty needle just under the skin; but also, slowly,
To come to love the night and her soft stars again.

The woods remained too, and the big wind
Teased through the needles of felled pines,
Red-grey cities which I will enter, a sprig
Of familiar weeds crushed in my wet fist.

And, between two vertebrae, a sliver of fear:
What remains of a death which passed quite near.
And rickety bridges into the bubbles of distance,
Which I walk, fairly firmly, in thinned file.

HOW ORPHEUS SANG

A thicket of song, with every note a rose;
A voice of copper, of fruit and foam; a space
Where every branch outstretches, lengthens and grows
All soft beneath the bark, as if to expose
Its blackened body to a woman's embrace.

The beasts of the field and forest scarcely sensed
The moment their blood congealed to mead. Yet here
They stand, the great with the small, all bristling, tensed;
Sculpted, it seems, where the silence has condensed,
A lake of light in every attentive ear.

In his singing, time is translated to sound,
Softened into the limpid, protean form
Of shallow water where red-dappled trout abound,
The speckled tints of flowered and grassy ground,
And the taste of sunlit soil, humid and warm.

And he sings his song in the gentle, pouring rain,
In the purple clover; the raw flesh pulsates
Under his skin; but his ears secretly strain
For a wiser voice to echo the refrain
Beneath the stone, where silence's first wave waits.

STRANGER

This is the river, slightly blue, ready to go quietly
Into its bend, where three green blades of pine
Are gradually rusting away; where the midstream
Turns the fish, gently nudging their fins.

The sandy bank rises unobtrusively,
Like the chance move of a hand, to slide
Below the fresh hem of a dense grove of poplars
Shivering in the wind from the other side.

His steps leave silent traces in the sand.
He moves pensively, merging like a stain
Into the leaves; then he reappears
On the sand, superfluous, with meekly dangling hands.

Birdsong has trickled down the silvery scales
Of the poplar grove. Fish and the first stipples
Of dusk swim in the river. The cool of evening, fresh
As a netful of shivering fish shaken from the mesh.

His steps measured, a little stiff,
He walks the wet sand: almost a marionette. As if
Suspended on the fear his next step might lift
Him from the landscape, long before the bend.

OPHELIA

The rivers rock her as they bear
Her body, white and swollen with water;
They swirl her lush and unkempt hair
Braided with twigs where branches have caught her.

The depths are caressed by two soft hands:
Beneath them, minnows uneasily flit;
Her neck is wreathed with water-weed strands;
Like rotting cherries, her lips have split.

Inquisitive raindrops sometimes spill
Into each sky-blue, wide-open eye,
And trickle from her lids until
A drifting cloud sponges them dry.

Sometimes a wind in the rushes will chase
A wave across the water – it slips
Like rippling laughter over her face:
The river is learning to smile with her lips.

The current carries no empty shell,
No water-shadow, futile and blind,
For another seeks her beauty's spell:
With death himself she lies entwined.

This is sensed by the shrieking crows,
The hollow reeds, and frost's first ashes
Along the banks; is known to the snows,
Its early flakes impaled on her lashes.

Ophelia, why not try to weep;
Alive with death, to sink anew,
And free your dead love from his keep –
Or does he still mean freedom for you?

Slow your progress: bridges quiver,
Sails are bathed in the heat of the sun.

Death in your flesh, the gurgling river
Beneath you: is your suffering done?

Surely, Ophelia, you did no wrong:
You're only weak, so the waters bear
Your body, your arms dangling along,
Twigs entangled in your hair.

But once you decay you will be saved,
As death within you forgets his desire –
Then give way to the tears you've craved,
And sink like a star to the depths of the mire.

WIND

Do you remember the wind, born once all green
Between the hair on Hammer Peak's head?
Your mother closed the shutters on the pines,
Unquiet to the bitter roots of their needles;
Darkness had fallen, too big for you,
Like a grown-up's clothes. But your mother carries a candle,
Her hand carefully guarding the flame on the stairs.
Wind. Every door in the house is barred,
Pine trees and tramps will stay outside in the wind,
But you're a good boy and mother will seal
Your little everyday waking with a kiss.

Angels guard my sleep, I pray,
Keep all evil dreams away.

For the night is big and the wind is beneath the sill,
The cones are falling, and the moon will be clean
And burnished by the wind, small and round.
You fell asleep, quite sure you would wake
In the morning. Like the wind. Like the wind.

PRAYER

Love, thy will be done
In these heavens, so terribly insecure,
As on earth. Now the season of colours, for
The south wind's hurried leafing, has begun.

Now the nights are blue and as soft as the skins
Of fruit, like shallow wells for the stars to fill.
Let people love one another as they will,
In provisional circles of little things.

Love, thy will be done
Here in these cities, stubbornly motionless,
Which cannot summon the strength to break and run,

Where the unwounded leaves still cast their shawls,
Between the people who live in happiness,
For they put their faith in ancient harbour walls.

REQUIEM FOR A MOTHER

Licht der Liebe! scheinest du denn auch Toten, du goldnes!
    – HÖLDERLIN

The winds clothe the sky over our city
And know nothing of poverty. But no winds
Ripple the mirrors of your dead eyes,
Halted, like a little flood, beneath the roots
Of a forked lime tree. Between you and the light
Lives earth. Look – you are walled into silence
Like a bird into light, together with the dead years,
Whose blood has clotted to berries of darkness under the vault.

I hear footsteps teeming like ants
And the flat fall of the leaves. Where is my boy,
With light's unfocused image in his inherited eyes?

Shoots of grass have riddled the russet soil.
You lie unmoving, your voice plundered,
Full to the eyes with love under seal.
Did you recognise these steps, once a boy's,
Cut short at the edge of your silence
As fish hold back before a shore?
He leans against the forked lime tree,
Facing your name. Brimful of words, like a bell.

He has stopped. Those steps grew from me.
Is that my boy, who has come of age between the great
Shattered windows of the unknown years?

Sleep on, walled so solidly into your silence, and listen
As you sleep to the little lizards basking in the sun
And the sprouting of the grass. The man once a boy has said
With an inherited voice: the tongue of the name of my love
Lives in the things which encircle love.
If I am no better for this (though goodness flows
Like the tide in little coves), at least I am richer,
Like a tree which is forced to leaf.

My boy. My eyes, wiped clean of death.
Happy, he turns and walks away. My boy.

A VOICE SINGING IN GARDENS

How can I hunt down the voice swimming out of me
Like a bird out of the sky, a stranger now,
Self-sufficient and conscious of its own existence,
The voice making fun of its homeland
Of blood and gentle ignorance, as it sings
Somewhere in its own pure sphere, which my wounded fingers
Cannot fumble after, and whose boundaries
My long-cheated gaze cannot grasp? (Perhaps at the top
Of the stair?) How can I hunt down the voice
Born once in the flesh of my first awakening
Like a weird, blind stranger, maturing faster,
The voice now singing in the green space
Of gardens on the far side of hearing, now transformed into a bird?

Timidly, afraid of breaking some law
I do not know, I sneak past the walls,
The latticed walls of reality, with the first signs
Of a numb fatigue in the movements of my limbs.
To whom can I confess this futile hunt, whom can I ask
In the plain of sun and blue tar,
On the bench under the avenue of petrified trees,
Whom can I ask about the voice in the gardens?
People lean their arms on their usual tables,
Dip bread into salt, laugh or go away,
Usually through the door, and disappear into themselves
Or without themselves. As for the dead, whom I am afraid
To ask in case they know much, too much,
They do not notice us as they concentrate on
Carefully dismantling their former fates,
Like watchmakers – they are outside the gardens, anyway.

And yet, perhaps, a tree is left in the wind,
A street, a brief ripening of permanence,
A few broken toys, and the voice is left,
A voice which once lived here
But now sings in gardens.

THIS GREAT BIG MOON

This great big moon which is just about to set,
Beautiful and superhumanly huge, in orange blood,
This sweet, unrounded miracle one black winter morning
Over the sharp karst of mouldering roof-spines,
Oh distant waiting of mine, this witnessed moon
Of honey and dust over rooms now asleep
Where the breath of lovers has misted the silence
On windows as brittle as ice on ponds,

A moon with no spectacles, gun or smile
Passes my life like a ship, somewhat solemnly,
As I stand here, stand here upon the shore,
My hands in my pockets, and do not move,
For I half-hate this moon, this great big moon
Which tells me: you're alone, and does not notice me.

RIDER

Fresco

Horse and lord of the bridle, surging as one
In the service of iron. The frightened grass
Has withdrawn its tiny tongues. And shivers run
Across the summer silence, tougher than glass.
The youth is movement, air is resistance won.

Eye to eye. Like water with water they slide,
Edgeless, into each other. Talons beneath
The belly, the dense hatred of flinty teeth.
The horse is lathered in sweat, its eyes are wide.

The lance suddenly ripe with the rider's weight
Above the dragon, as horse and master rear.
Beneath the moss, the earth is quaking in fear,
Has turned to stone. The dragon has turned to slate.

FOUR EPITAPHS

To a Dancer

The secret of our parting is closed into the moment
You fumbled, like someone suspicious and blind,
For the back of the known. A movement which blossomed
Into the rose-coloured foam of a childhood orchard.
A movement in which you peeled off the shadow
Heavier than you, for truer to earth.
And now, those who love you can dream of a fiery
Black rose beneath a hill of blue, transparent ice.

To a Fighter

There lies an undreamed dream of death disarmed,
There a little earth is senselessly armed.
Pressed into the earth with the red-hot signet ring
Of a faithless death, he sinks ever deeper, and does not hear
The fall of leaves riddled with late light;
He sinks ever deeper, like a ship holed by a bolt of fear –
Abandoned by its crew, suddenly loathsome to the light
By the law of cruel metamorphosis.

To a Sailor

In the end, the sea smoothed away its wrinkles.
He remained, cradled in the warm lap of the current.
His arms outflung, he listens hard; turning
On a rose of drowned winds, he dips
Like a blunted compass needle, seeking
A course for a shore.

To a Singer

Here lies the sworn translator of a green
Tongue. Dust has settled his deserted lips.
Has anyone ever looked death in the ear
As if into an iron well, an echo well,
To see his voice turn to stone and drop to shatter
The silence at the bottom, but the bottom does not exist?

THE HOME OF THE SWANS

You see, I know that there, in the home
Of blind tenderness, in the lost paradise of the unspoken,
Live the swans, bursting into bloom on a green
Mirror, beautiful with the light which we forgot
When we became dangerously strong, when we
Became arrows faster than ourselves.
Tell me the way to the home of the swans
Which sometimes appears in the roots of your smile
Like a dream of a shore painlessly merged
With the blue light where breathe the swans.
Perhaps I must slowly disarm myself
Like a soldier who wants to bathe in a river
On a summer afternoon, laying down his armour
In the dusty grass, drunk with sunshine.
And then fall like a scream in a stone shell,
Until I break the pane of awareness.
Perhaps I would see swans flying up into the sky,
Armed with a beauty stronger than our duration.
Perhaps I would know the way back, to surprise you
With the picture of a swan smuggled through in my eyes,
Eyes you would recognise. Or perhaps I would stay
There in the home of our tenderness,
Dead, forever convulsed in glorious horror,
Smeared with the blood of swans.

SUMMER

Great, yellow fires blaze at every crossing,
The dangerous fires of midday. Don't look back.
Birds are dying in the burning lace of foliage,
Trapped in the glare of white-hot mirrors
At the crossroads. Don't look back.
A crimson poppy opens on the peeling
Lips of earth: a poisoned summer. Don't look back.
Don't give in to midday. If you give in to midday
You won't live to see the night.

Beauty of hell, presence of what is not,
Drumming of a hundred rains way beyond hearing;
This is the hour a drowsy god lay down,
And wisdom left his forehead, fully-armed.
Summer.

This equilibrium, this leaden weigh-beam of years,
This nodding dream beneath a clotted bloodstream
Of flora, this life of dust in wells, stalemate,
Is an evil dream whose flames will die tonight
In the green fire of the sea.

Walk on, don't look back. Now midday's yellow fires
Are blazing everywhere, at every crossing,
The great lie of the lethal equilibrium,
Spring cut short and autumn denied,
The scorching resin which seals the passages of sense,
The fires of midday. Do not look back, unless you want
To stay forever at the focus of a vicious light
Which will devour your shadows, the tiny shadows
You need in order to vanish with dignity.

From the cycle 'Orpheus on Deck'

OF EURYDICE

No one prevented me plunging my voice,
Plated in violet silver, into your darkness,
Your thick darkness devoid of time;
But my voice melted on your sweaty palms, choked
On black feathers from the strata of dead birds,
And vaporised on the coals of wisdom in your eyes,
And now, gnawed to the bone by the walls' invisible sneers,
I return alone.

Lords of the back of duration, had love
Not suffused my crimson fear, as the
South wind is drenched with the smell of the sea,
I would not have knocked at the doors of forbidden return.
But you let me tell the sands of dead time, and
Spattered me with your knowing, silent laughter
When I believed my blood-heavy eyes.

I was alone, you see. And I walked
Your corridors, only to stay so.
But still I robbed your darkness of a little light
And touched your tranquil lips and limbs,
To understand the senseless meaning of my loss.
Eurydice, unravelled like a tree into its roots,
Lasts on outside me, without a farewell wave.

And now, gnawed to the bone by the walls' invisible sneers,
I dig my nails into my dumbstruck, ashy palms,
To leave as I came, with dignity,
Not crying out, nor running for the doors of the sun,

Afraid, and hideously enriched.

From the cycle 'Orpheus on Deck'

SONG FOR THE DEAD

Nobody dies too late, O lords of the far side
Of curiosity, nobody ever dies too late
To find an open door. Someone will be waiting to wipe
The blood in silence from his frightened lips, to name
Him once and for all. This much I know – I who, through
A game of miracle, can breathe deeply once again, beneath
A sky furrowed like a shell by the knives of wind, though
I wished to break the bread of death with clean fingers.

There's still a lot left on this side of curiosity:
The tarnished silver dripping from your mirrors,
The marrow of wisdom sucked with toothless gums
From the broken bones of time, a barren light
Grown old in the eyes of amber, corridors
Of resinous tears, red walls of silence which open
Only to a knocking from within, the naked
Roots of what was once a dream, fruitlessly watered
From without by the tears of the unknowing,
Oh all I clumsily called your sort of happiness,
Perplexed by your tranquillity, perplexed by your roses
Fleshily unfolding by inner moonlight.

Afraid, I underestimated you, O lords of the
Back of this duration. Forgive me my mistake.
For who could have known the price of the power
Of staying silent about it all? Who could have known the
Secret rule of our common game: that there is no winner,
For the stakes cannot be changed? Oh, now I know
That you listen for the motion of the same sea,
Only with sharper ears. You fear the same gods.

But now I no longer know your sort of happiness,
And so I respect you, unknown lords
Of my love, who stayed behind in the long tunnel,
Weightless and blue as will-o'-the-wisp,
Named once and for all, outside me.

From the cycle 'Orpheus on Deck'

WICK

You know me, night: the flame of a candle. I
Am the flickering shadow's root, I am heat;
The air shivers, casting the shadows high,
But even now the light refuses to die
While an unknown measure remains incomplete.

For the short time I exist, my task I know:
To express upon the walls each object's shade;
Darkness is but a handful of blackish snow
Melting on the fire of my miracle's glow,
A wound I slash with my incandescent blade.

You know me: in bitter rooms condemned to burn
Surrounded by aging things – this is my fate.
I live in your thick-massed bark, a golden worm:
For the brief eternal world which I confirm,
Everything that I devour I recreate.

You know me, night, while my blood's incisors gnaw
Away the brief pride of my height; as I warm
The shadows over my voice, their voices yaw;
Ear of yellow fire, and fire of yellow straw,
I am fertile beneath the walls of the storm.

II

FRESCO

Angry angel on the verge of pure flame,
The contorted air ignites at your gaze, which recalls
The forgotten: you emerge from the wall,
Armed and grim, as you once emerged from a night
When it was complete, despising the illusory
Pattern of stars, for you now seared
With the perilous beauty that inseminates time.
Angry angel on the verge of pure flame,
If you step forth the wall will crumble,
But your splendid miracle will stay.

Forgive me my weakness.

Angry angel with your smile of invisible light,
Night is now tame behind your shoulder
Which bears an arm untired by its gesture
Of warning. But who will stay buried beneath
This solid wall, if you should step forth?
Filled with yourself, you do not explain your existence,
Just like the wind, which hides in fear of you
Inside the little eye of the candle. Angry angel,
I have come from a space beyond these walls to seek
The golden honeycomb between the jaws of your silence.

Forgive me my mortality.

Angry angel on the verge of pure flame,
The night is large from which you emerged,
I fear lest I disappear before you notice me.

Lead me not into fear.

BYZANTIUM

Image on a golden ground, innocent blush
Of an aging sun, I sing you this because I love you,
Dead miracle, detested beauty whose marble bones
Lie buried beneath the grass and cypress trees;
I think of you with pride, hoarding a little of your
Wise gold deep in my eyes, which sprouted
Like flowers out of the earth, having absorbed
Your last few drops of blood, cruel mistress.
I hate the hatred that dawns like the premature
Child of impotent spite in the disbelieving eyes
Which drift from the forests of the setting sun.
Oh, how they despised you, miraculous dead light!

> *Here the domes of palaces*
> *Rose like golden chalices,*
> *Whilst in the lands to the west*
> *Everything simply regressed:*
> *Gangs of malodorous knights*
> *Whose pastime was hunting lice.*

Beauty is never forgiven, nor is a lonely wisdom,
O torn frontier with two wide worlds flowing
Through your blood. For you were still heavy
With marble gods who had fallen asleep, eyes open, beneath
The thin grass. And the blue-lipped shores were the same,
After all, under the same sun. The same olives.
But all was softer now, with an ominous ripeness.
The ripeness of the agave. Like the gazes of the emperors
On the steps. Perhaps with a touch of ennui.
Too many images, noble and cruel, drowned in the pools of
Beautiful women's eyes. And the walls have started to sing.
But the borders withdraw like an obedient sea.

> *A rabble of western knaves*
> *Come stumbling out of their caves.*
> *At writing Charlemagne's quick,*
> *He knows some arithmetic.*

Grown old now, our sun sinks low,
A bubble the breezes blow.

Twofold wisdom, grove of silver cypress trees
Misty with incense – cruel mistress,
You befuddled, rank by rank, even the visored eyes
Of barbarians with crosses on their famished bellies.
They raped you, then you ate them, horses and all.
You, dead light, first heard the distant drumming
Of a dusty, dreadful green cavalry on the flank
Of your world. All that remains in the end is a city
On a neck of sea, encircled by the crimson eyes of fire,
And gazes teeming feverishly in her towers
And cast into the callous void of a sea
Without sails. They forgot you, beauty of the world,
Because they wanted to. Your blood be on their heads.

We're not uncaring, far from it –
But face those guns of Mahomet?
We'll send the politest of tears
To comfort those Greek buccaneers.
And why doesn't Constantine call
Those priests of his onto the wall?

The blood streamed into the sea. The fish fled.
Sublime dead miracle, trapped in the pupils of time.

SMEDEREVO

We have built a citadel, Ivoje, a citadel of stone,
And dipped the shadows of the four-cornered towers
In the wide grey river. The citadel is on the right bank
And the wind on the left. Autumn has come
And behind us the woods have rusted in the rain.
Men keep watch at night over the heavy gates,
Bearing weapons, dark in their armour, like stag-beetles,
And warm their frozen hands over the crimson fire.
We wait, and twenty-four towers wait with us,
Exposed to time as to the rain, all of us together.
I think we will never be forgotten, we who watch
From the last citadel on the right bank of the river,
Although we will not turn to stone beneath the towers;
It is enough that we are the ones who wait, who strain our ears
For the echo of a thousand hooves growing in the night
Beneath the indifferent stars. Our Lord the Prince
Drinks wine as golden as the carp in the river,
But his beard has turned grey like the glory of his fathers;
May the Lord give him an end before the end.
We are the last. If we fall asleep here beneath the towers,
Who will wake us? The fires are burning low.
The citadel is on the right bank, and the wind on the left.

LETTER FROM THE KNIGHT SINADIN

who fell in the Battle of Angora
in the Year of Our Lord 1402

We crossed the narrow neck of sea, blue, dancing,
And swam into stone, into sand mad with winds,
Into a sun without sky, strangers among strangers.
The sea, flowering in light and foam, stayed
On the other side, behind our hearts. We rode through
Weeks overgrown with the dark foliage of roads,
Rutted roads, the pain of hooves, and evenings
Which sucked the sun from our scorching armour.
O fate, how you are peopled with wonders!
Our enemy was unknown, as were the women
Whose smiles stayed melting on the tracery grilles
Of houses girdled by walls and silence, still
Unforgotten. But when the drumming doubled,
And when the dry earth went mad with fear,
We struck eyes eaten out by the wind:
Then we recognised the hatred in the future victors,
While our eyes were the great empty sky.
Why did we fill it with the blood and iron of arrows?
And now we retreat and close our ears
To hide the sound of the grass growing up like knives
On the sand of our graves.

DEATH WITH A FALCON

The yellow sound of horns stabbing among the leaves,
Somebody's laughter dissolves in sunlight. The joy of thirst
Ripened in the saddle. Just before the clearing the branches
Unfold, like hands from eyes
In a capricious game. And then they saw:

A black bird hovering in the blue circle of sky.

Nobody smiles but the Prince, who knew.
Nobody but the Prince, whose face is furrowed
With a bloody wisdom, the Prince whose eyes
Are wide with remembrance, grey as the salt sand
Of swallowed time. The Prince lifts his gaze,
Slowly, like an over-heavy shield on a wounded arm.
And then he looses the falcon.

Later they said: the earth shook
When the bird disappeared and the Prince fell from his horse
And the falcon kept circling and would not return.

If, in the end, one has to die, it is fine
To die with a falcon, one's own falcon,
Circling and looking for a black bird in the blue
Circle of sky, mad and blind with light.

THE DANUBE BY SMEDEREVO

for I. and B.

Pison, the colour of dirty silver, flowing from Paradise
On the way to Donji Milanovac and beyond,
On the way to melt down its name in the shimmer
Of the thirsty sea, cold Danube burdened with memories
And metres of mud, furrowed by steamers
As the morning sky by the wind – the river passes by the fortress,

But we are in the fortress, my Prince, a few friends
In this swamp of wind and autumn sun, absorbed in our game
Between the shadows of birds swooping through empty lancets,
Down onto your stone, up into your sky; we call to one another
Amid the wrenched molars of towers, levelled crenellations,
And the shadows of archers carbonised into crystals of air.

We are in a defenceless fortress, among stones
Still lukewarm from your last summer, my Prince;
In this shell of stone, among words scattered to the four corners
Of the rose-garden of winds, over the rubbish-heap of years,
We are absorbed in a game of recognition; this spell
Of an afternoon in the double zodiac of your towers,

This short impossibility of death as long as we recognise
Both ghosts: that old fire which settles upon our shoulders,
And you, lost in thought at the window, with the whistle
Of a shunting engine in a siding, as you watch
Pison, the colour of dirty silver, flowing from Paradise
With all its barges on the way to its beginning.

RESAVA

How long can a guard hold out
In the gorge, trained for an imaginary
Eternity, and forgotten in the shingle roll
Of ebbing splendour, in a night of conflicting signals?

Warrior saints, angels of defeat
With weapons of men, a blunted flame
Sings on your wings, between walls
Where the echo hunts a shadow, the shadow hunts a gaze
Staring at a perfect point, and empty.

The icy shadow of a nut tree, and a rose
Beneath the wall. Winds shimmer,
Great thirsty caravans of air
Over the ravine beneath the guard;
                                 pollen mixed with dust
Is falling on your armour, sentinel angels.

And an alien radiance
In the halos over your pensive heads: the time is
Growing inside you, the taste is changing in the fruit.

But battle is booming, fire is singing
In the clear space of your hearing, imagined
For the few words I struggle to remember
At the moment of waking,

Bitter-lipped, amnesiac,
As I stand before a sentry who demands a password
In the language of my clan.

1804

A great mill grinds through dead of night,
A black mill, churning the grey race of eternity,
A shaking mill grinds through dead of night,
A wordless mill, sifting a miracle,
A mill without a miller.

It grinds a gritty, bloody grist,
It grinds the centuries of ungnawed gristle,
It grinds the flame and the frightened bells,
It grinds the shores all sheathed in fire,
It grinds the horses, grinds the riders,
It grinds the rope and grinds the stake,
It grinds the rain and grinds the sun,
It grinds the Supper on Blackbird Field,
It grinds the birds and the burning wheat,
It grinds the faces eaten by time,
It grinds its own biting fate
To the fine grist of revolt.

In through the walls, beneath the pierced eyes of the stars,
Over the thatch of black and stinging moss,
In through the raped door and the spit-gobbed windowpanes –
Eight score horsemen, four by four,
Over the scent of blood already changing
To flowers which deck legends and graves,
Over the children sliced open with knives,
Sliced open like unripe fruit
Cast aside at the glorious banquet of time,
Horsemen, foul winged horsemen,
Ground, unnoticed, to grist.

It will grind you too, you who are bound round with fear,
It will grind you too, all you hard-eyed heroes,
It will grind your fingers, your little routines,
It will grind your wizened god inside you,
This mill without a miller.

For it grinds a gritty, bloody grist,
It grinds its own blinded pain,
It grinds the tears and the ancient books,
It grinds the steel of hate and grinds the cinders,
It grinds the darkness, grinds the one who grows the grain,
It grinds the spirit of frightened contempt,
It grinds the distances, grinds the bloodstained dresses,
It grinds its own cuckolded fate
To the edible grist of light.

Without a miller, at dead of night.

PRINCIP ON THE BATTLEFIELD

to my father

Emerging onto an empty field,
With no wedding ring, no coat of many colours,
No Blessed Prince's tent,

There was thunder last night, a short squall,
The scent of the limes richer for the short memory of lightning,

My hand against my forehead, this wind
Five centuries heavy, shimmering, huge,
The banner under which I stumble,

At a street corner with a view of the river,
Where time starts to sing in the voices of old men
Blind with black sun,

With no armour, I mingle between the passers-by
And the gilded shadows,
With no option now, I stand on a empty field
Where the hooves of battle pound.

I raise my hand:

– Let all be blessed and just –
And fire.

REQUIEM

for the seven hundred from the church in Glina

1

I cannot stay silent; the walls stayed silent
And crumbled. One, I carry them all inside me, unspoken,
Overgrown with my adulthood, their faces
Rotted away. I cannot evict them from the
Infinite glassy space of the sleepless nights.
They are not grass. At night, from within,
They cautiously tap at the trembling panes
Of my eyes; all dead, and all their throats
Have blossomed into roses. I cannot stay silent
About this colony in my blood, for I am one,
And they were more than seven hundred then.

2

Within the walls, behind the bolted doors,
Filled with a hideous waiting, as if with sand,
Empty-handed, soft before the blades, aware,
Beneath a vault convulsed with dawning horror . . .
I, once a boy, imagine the first dull thrust
Which frees the warm, dark blood from the body
Of the first: treacherous blood, quick to flee.
And I hear the first scream, wet with reddish foam
From a throat whose songs are forever slashed,
Whose words are unspoken, split in half
Like green apples in its darkness.
Steel. And the first, waiting for his companions
In a death shamefaced and roomy enough
To receive them. Here are their eyes, here their eyes
Are extinguished two by two, lifeless lights in a morning street,
But the horror is left inside like grit in a cube of ice.
Blood, inquisitive, stripped, flows across
The flagstones. Steel in flesh, steel which trembles still
In the sleeplessness of one who was once a boy.
They fell into blood, their senses crushed,

And could not hear the next, the one with branded eyes,
Or the one pruned with steel like a tree,
Between the walls grown thick with screams
And rich with fear. And the red mouths
Of fresh wounds were mute, filled with blood.
There they lay, abased, stripped of self,
Stripped of all but death, red, sticky,
Slaughtered, slaughtered, slaughtered.

3

I cannot stay silent; the walls stayed silent
And crumbled. But the ones from the church, the ones
Who are dead, have not yet fallen asleep. They lie awake,
Unbidden, in one who was once a boy. I cannot evict them
Into the space of wind where the church once stood,
Where the weeds grow all red with their blood.
So let them stay, awake, unbidden, for they would despise me
If I were to try to sing them to sleep.

CHAMBER POEM FOR A CITY

These words sing of miraculous, sooty stone
Which opens like a hand, unfolds to form
A single flower whose scent is fire,
A flower on the lips of rivers, sooty stone,
Searing bead in a rosary forever between
The restless, frazzled fingers of time.

1

I dream I understand rivers; my hearing silts thick
With bone-bitter sand. I dream I understand wind
And see walls of fossilised light, see a fortress
Looted by time, the root of a copper rose of sun
Which remembers far too much. I open my eyes,
Then close them again, it's all the same: the city remains.

A wound remains, branded into the skin of ages,
A pensive headland, riddled like an ant-hill,
Conquerors' skulls which the rivers have opened
Like shells, then covered with shingle;
A sketch in the sands of the tide, wiped and repeated
In a game of patience. A city remains.

2

Scarred scarp, skyline of scoffing scaffolds, screeching
Escutcheons: a boar stabbed with the arrow of waking,

Belgrade, my white swan,

Flames in the dark, the blood of nameless chroniclers,
A clatter of arms which pierces the skin of the river,

Belgrade, my white swan,

Defenders wiped from the regimental rolls,
A white swan hanging from every chandelier, blood which can
Only be washed from the streets by gentleness and hate.
All that remained was to imagine gardens –
The rest is known.

3

These words sing of miraculous, sooty stone
Which opens like a hand, unfolds in the wind.
These words sing of a city on the banks of two rivers
And a single time the colour of blood and sun,
These words written slowly in spring.

The body of an eternally youthful god beside the river,
A smile on his missing face, eaten away to the cinders of time.
Though his breast is riddled, ringing bronze,
And his arms sink heavily into the soil, like roots,
Burned bronze, a flute for the green breeze,
Pierced by the shoots of wide-eyed plants,
The tortured torso of an eternally youthful bronze god,
Swathed in light and swaying blossom,
Dreams of an age of tenderness beside the river.

III

Melissa

Twenty-Four Fragments

1   BEES

Melissa, your body dissolving to bees, the awed
And fearful flowers that share your secret, pure
Fire, the turbid grapes of eyes mature
When your sight is severed, like an umbilical cord;

From the far side of darkness, Melissa, the gold
Of your blood pours scorn upon the god who wore
Me down with the burden of presence – O secret of your
Metamorphosis, suddenly buzzing thousandfold,

Blood the colour of summer, whose humming lingers
All afternoon, dripping from blades of light
Beyond my sight, as I break my dirty fingers

On the hideous bulk of your wall, till these
Torn hands bear fruit, my speechless words grow white
As milk, as your body, Melissa, turning to bees.

2   THE SECRET OF THE LOAVES

I want to make your secret mine, Melissa,
For I have fallen in love with your kind of bliss;
Within me another unchronicled city crumbles,
Within me live empty houses without numbers,

Within me the roots of a black moon have spread
Through sinewed strata of inherited dread,
Within me a redheaded struggle, an antlered pride
Stabs in vain where the landscape of breath is tied

The tightest; and yet your secret's splendid shout,
Melissa, shakes the hills if I think about
It – surely it underlies, exquisite and mellow,

This circle rimmed by an icy sea, and prefaces,
Perhaps, an even lovelier legend of genesis,
Leavening loaves huge, crustless and yellow.

3   STAR

All round us, Melissa, fields once used to sway
In a pure breeze. But they are beyond recall:
Only in our blood does a boat still stay
Under sail, its crew long gone – and this may all

Be no more than a wish reduced to an ember which still
Refuses to blaze, to the banner of time which flies
Inside me, to the flesh of my moment which will
Not ripen: an ancient wish, which constantly drives

Me to summon a memory unknown to these angry rings
Of cliffs, to christen dangerously everyday things
With the names of flowers, fruit, or metals that gleam;

Dance on a knife-tip, features of evil, I shy
At the meaning of the image as old as a dream:
The star cannot hear the frenzied falconer's cry.

4   NORTH WIND

Meanwhile, Melissa, you smile your absent smile:
Lapped in death outwitted with godly guile,
Beneath the cities which, through a misty pall,
Still feel your smile, like a sleeper sensing the fall

Of autumn rain, as the constellations try in vain
To kindle their sodden fires in a thickening sky
Confused and high, as in the empty domain
The north wind slowly opens its lashless eye,

An eye which consumes the love in those who defy
It; O strength with no everyday face, who remembers
You here in this everyday darkness, rainy and late,

When things are hard and silent, and people die,
Their consciousness suddenly redundant, like embers
Of ancient fire dumped in a wet grate?

5   HORSE

O stars transformed to beasts, O beasts transformed
To stars, a horse is charging towards me, the horse,
Evil and proud, of the slaughtered marauder who stormed
With his breastplate of bronze the terrified altar doors;

A horse of a breed long dead, heavy and broad,
Bearing no rider – he fell long ago in the mud,
His eyes wide with a curse, a star of blood
In his gullet. I fear, as his horse thunders toward

Me, my voice will shrink to a wisp of terror, the scream
Of an empty hall – O stars now beasts, O beasts
Now stars which stream through duration's splintered gate,

I stand before you hideously whole, released
From the power of fission to blood and flame, and wait
For hooves that pound from a louring plain, from a dream.

6   WALL

This is the wall, Melissa; behind its stones,
A garden which bees, your body, fill with their drones.
But I see no door, and birds, their feathers the red
Of death, sprout from the sky and swoop on my head

To peck at the true dream asleep in each eye;
My dream is bread and in it you are a rose,
But the bread is behind the wall in your buzzing glade,
I see red birds on the foreheads of passers-by

Though they know of nothing, Melissa, and fill their bowls
With the everyday food of the living, for error must
Prevail; the wall was unscathed by the scream I thrust

Between its stones like a knife, and now the blade
Is broken, a bird is flying about my ears:
Melissa, your garden wall is a wall of tears.

7   RECOGNITION

Legend, resonant rose in a pestilent breeze,
Forest walled in with the flames of deathless leaves,
You fill me with crimson pain, for you are torn
Flesh buzzing with bees, where a wonder is born

Of blood sucked from the flowers which decorate
Your southern garden, of salt from the tear-filled eyes
Of time: a miraculous honeycomb, which is fate;
Your wound gives me pain, but to feel it implies

I'm living my fate – O rumorous fire, ablaze
With seed, in this star I know you, the first to sear
Through the evening; perhaps I know you here

In this doorless, windowless room, with only the hum
Of silence, fire – this, and the clock's dumb
Beat, and your eyes, fire – their fate-rich gaze.

8   FACE

Look, on this wall a stain is being born,
A green archipelago of tiny flowers
Of damp, the face of one drowned with no one to mourn
Him, an eyeless, mouthless face, a face with no powers,

A face which the jaws of time have defiled and gnawed
With craven callousness; whence that face which beseeches
From the wall of your garden? Who has immured
My fear's mirror, the verdigris of my features

Turned to you like the sky in a handful of rain?
When your voice merged with the legible mesh of my blood,
Melissa, I stripped off the pestilent rags of my fears

Until, defenceless and free, I understood
Your secret. We're not alone now, O monstrous stain,
O wall, O secret: another's eyes can see us.

9   MAN

A man with no shoulders, taking the shape of his flight,
O wind-borne rattle, O reek of sweat and fright,
A man transformed to his screaming, bruised and bent,
Bearing no weapon, bemedalled with age-old contempt,

Running across a sandy plain, his slight
Body stumbling, far too breathless and light,
The sun swims in the wind, its colour is black,
The hunters draw closer: faceless, the man looks back,

Beneath the black sun the sand is searing –
O rattle in the wind, louder, nearing –
Slower, sobbing, the man still tries to flee,

From the sand a city rises, sirens blare,
And I wake, my pain swathed in a sudden glare,
And hear his panting. He's gone to ground in me.

10   WAKING

And yet I know all round us there once was a sky
Refracted inside us, Melissa, like a beam
Of pure light. But this is forgotten; O by-
Gone sense of words with the taste of lushness and dream –

Like your name growing leaves in our blood, Melissa, dense
With the rustle of a magic tree, with the scents
Of forbidden fruit, a sky which lacks the unease
Of discovered distance, ancient and cool as the seas

Filled with ships where we sang, armed with ourselves;
But the ships are gone, our throats are dry and tense,
And forgetting has come, bearing the silt of migration,

To the cracked and windy rooms where this time dwells,
And I wake, in the heavy armour of a nation
Which knows of courage but cannot remember its sense.

14   SOUTH

Maybe the south, that warm, violet sea,
Riddled with windfall stars between the tree-
Clad shores, their droves of scented pine ablaze,
The tinder of light; and all those mariners' graves,

Their sailors at rest, eroded to crystals of salt;
Maybe that sun, forged without a fault
By the strokes of well-designed gods, maybe the trees
Which bear transparent, steam-dense winds that tease

Beneath your skin, inebriating and stinging;
Maybe that land of gracious beasts, which raise
Their heads, hornless and horned, to hear the singing,

The homeland of springs which mutter words, then grow
Opaque as fable, as the dark, imagined gaze
Which sees something in me, but deep down below.

15   SUMMER

Summer, my troubled dream of cool, black
Rain, when shallow rivers, losing their reason,
Forget their aims and shrink into sand: the season
The earth splits like a fevered lip, with a crack

That evaporates in the light, and the metaphrase
Of a resonant wind to droning swarms of flies;
Everything under this forest roof could blaze,
Though this means ripeness; but when I close my eyes –

Summer, a cell of glass where I wait for death:
No courage, just fear of noise, of a crack in my shell,
As I wait, mature, in a cube of sterile hell,

Ever hotter, and hear the rain outside – until
The walls collapse, getting me drunk on a breath
Of unearned coolness: but by another's will.

Voices of the dead. But not dead voices. Who
Can hear them? Rain on the copper gates of dawn. The cool
Of an overgrown garden, its nightingales held in a web of flowers.
I was the void between the lines, missing for hours

Down by the river, for days: it's all the same to me,
For this is a time outside this time, and the river is high
And wide. It flows with ancestral blood. But how am I
To swim upstream? Has anyone ever reached the sea?

O dead, upon the bank I found a house. With no
Rafters or roof-tree, abandoned in haste. And a thin thread
Of smoke was braided into the mist, which started to grow

Thicker. A half-built house. Then winter suddenly broke
And, frightened by the force of the storm, a window woke
Me. Who can hear their voices, the voices of the dead?

17   VOICES OF THE DEAD II

Somewhere far away, a fire flares in the night.
Behind it another. A third. Until there's a blazing mass
Of moths on the rim of night. A clear swathe of light,
A gold ring on a dream. It's finished. No one may pass.

Before the house the chestnut's leaves are falling in fear
And people say: it's autumn. An army is camped upon
The distant hills, Melissa, an army huge and dead.
Tense and breathless, I listen alone for a bugler. Instead

Of the blare of copper, I hear the early snows as they powder
The empty woods. But still the ring of fire blazes.
Earth smoothes a frown from her pensive brow, and razes

Cities to the ground. But still the fires burn on.
A gold ring around a dream. Did anyone hear
A bugler? He's blowing behind the silence, and silence is louder.

18 VOICES OF THE DEAD III

Melissa, to these ears the voices of the dead
Will always be dumb, and this is part of the game, a law
Poured into my wine, crumbled into my bread,
Carved with a red knife into the studded door

I am forever staring at, for what is to come
Lies on the other side. Their voices are not in the hum
Of your bees, which dissolve before me into the scented leaves
Like droplets of gold, and not beneath the silken eaves

Of the fir-wood risen where the mountainside once bled.
They're outside the game, Melissa, outside whatever I do.
I know the way to your garden: I could struggle through,

Armed with what I do not have. But not with a scream,
Nor with a knife. And no one can help me, alive or dead.
O hideous beauty: game without a go-between!

19 VOICES OF THE DEAD IV

Voices of the dead. Distant. But still they stay.
Voices of the dead. Who can hear them? The colour
Of old gold, perhaps, and a leaden ocean's spray.
Or perhaps mature as a gathering storm, ever-fuller,

Tensing. Or still with an unknown disease. It's all the same.
The colour of war, a bluish rattle, dust. With the slight
Hiss of a shell, held against the ear one bright
Summer's day. It's all the same: they're outside the game.

Voices. Words that drone just like a spinning wheel
From bedside tales, from pure dream-time disguised as the real.
Voices of the dead. But not dead voices. I lie at

Night, awake. Quiet, but not as they are quiet.
When I fall asleep, I dream of drums again.
Great, dark, gaping drums, beneath the rain.

20 MORNING

An age-old morning: the gods all show the same
Face in the caustic daybreak, immobile and cold,
All wet with others' tears, all green with mould,
Their smiles revealing beweaponed gums; no aim

To this morning – oh, the biting walls of this room
I must leave as usual and go among men to resume
Ancient migrations, with no hope of conclusion,
Through things whose presence, like stars, sows confusion;

A merciless morning, rain blue-voiced and raw
At the window, experience shackling my movements. While
Each morning I am weaker, the gods just smile

With their teeth; as I grow less, they stay the same:
Their cursed strength is my unknowing, this poor
Blood; my forgetting, these eyes, these hands that maim.

21 SLAVERY

O grubby god, O slavery to this voice,
This glass, this windowpane, this flower, this blade,
For a flower is only fire till it touches my hand,
A knife is a knife, and all is outside me, arrayed,

O grubby god, O slavery to this voice,
To this hearing of mine which lags behind the real
Sound like a wounded hunter, mocked by a band
Of invisible birds, to these eyes of mine which wheel

Sunflower-heavy and slow, with their imperfection;
This slavery of presence, of learned motion,
Of mirrors and faces, time is a fire where burn

My bones, O grubby god, while my journey's direction,
Its sense, trails behind me like the ocean,
Embroidered with roses of foam, behind the stern.

22   QUESTIONS

Triumphal arches sculpted in the wind, O who
Passed through you in pride? O writing on the water, blue
Phalanx of irises from a forgotten summer, how
Can I look back and not be blinded by your cascade?

O vain migration into things which cannot be found
Within the snowed-over frontiers of memory, raids on the black
And golden towers at the ends of this world which is bounded
By knowledge, defeats strangely blissful when I come back

As a pillager, wounded, and hideously enriched! But now
My summer is drawing near, gilded and late, in the shade
Of long, echoing corridors stretching empty ahead,

How can I look back and escape the retaliation
For the terrible hunt, the knife-ploughed gardens, the dead
Birds caught in the force-field of my imagination?

25   AN EVERYDAY SORCERER

I cast a solemn spell on the rain, the cool, dark
Rain, a spell to force the shoots to pierce the earth
To the core with a glittering inner pain, before they embark
Upon the adventure of air, upon the adventure of birth

And growth; I cast a spell on the rain, and hear them breathe
Behind me, all the living and all the dead who still
Hope for a pure harvest. See, the skies are wreathed
In foam the colour of a louring wind, and spill

Their first drops: oh fateful blunder, a rain of glowing
Blood, the woods are burning, the scorched earth cries –
And now, my empty, futile hands raised to defend

Myself, I'm all alone, afraid of death, the price
I must pay, in a blaze of burning leaves, for not knowing
The name of the murky power I did not comprehend.

28   SOLEMN WORDS

What must I do with you, dark and solemn words
Which spring from the brow of a calm, starry night,
From a cypress, a clear wind, the harmonious quiet
Of familiar beauty; what must I do with you, words

Which bloom like a wound, blind to ruins old
And new; surely not toss you into the holes
Eaten by black lichen in space's flesh,
Where the spiders of fear weave their drunken mesh?

Wretched, solemn words, you'll have no weight
And hang in the air, unworthy, lacking the most
Basic power: of breaking, like sea on a coast;

Wretched, solemn words, you'll disintegrate
To skeins of mist, naked and absurd –
O words, phantoms from an unsung world!

29   THE LOVELIEST BIRD

Melissa, body changing to bees,
Yellow fire whose meaning has slipped away
But I can sense in these broken nights of unease,
As a blind man senses the bird of a summer's day

In old, shadow-ripe gardens, when wind strands
Its thick, rustling silk through the dark hands
Of cypress branches: sad and wheezing with age,
He's felled, perhaps, by a pebble hurled in rage

At the loveliest bird; O fatuous death, for they
Who shoot at the loveliest bird can never aim
True, though blind men die in gardens, unknown,

Felled by spiteful slings, as the blind stone
The blind; but the bird flutters sedately away
Like a ship of legend, and sings on high, like a flame.

30   ROSE / TORCH

Your bees, Melissa, flee from my bloody-coloured
Torch, lit in the hubbub of a night
When death looms larger, and in the depths of the cupboard
A jug begins to shudder, like the light

In a pupil pulsating with fear, like a lily in wheat
At the touch of a twisted summer's furnace heat,
The season the jaws of a mindless menace wrench
At the necks of cities, and pallid seas clench

The spasms of searing shores; O torch, so small
In the night, you blazed as the muscle, tender but taut,
Of a budding rose was pierced by fear, then caught

Flame, cremating an unknown bee at its core –
One burning bee, the night the wave-battered wall
Of death is breached, exposing her ravaged shore.

31   THE FLOWER OF BEGINNING

And still, Melissa, you smile your thousand smiles from the bright
Gardens loud with bees behind my hearing, where grow
Your great transparent hives, gorged with the honey of light,
Bitter with oblivion; where gyres, huge and slow,

A bitter sun through memory's louring sky, a sun
Which brings a purer waking, which brings still purer dreams
Than the dreams and waking of this death; O heavy honey-
Comb of ancient sense, which nowadays only gleams

For an instant, between the blades of fear, just like the toll
Of a bell whose clapper men have wrenched away, an old
Sound which travels on alone, forgotten but whole –

It is the voice of a bee, Melissa, buzzing gold
On a flower fresh as genesis, wet with morning rain,
Unfurling its petals beyond a sky of dust and pain.

IV

FOUR PSALMS

1

I'll make you a land

From water as light and pure as your breath,
From the bright dust of the highroad, from the fire
That breathes into the frozen flesh of roses,
From the ravaged blood of air,

From the nourishing ashes of sleep, from the roots
Of felled hope, from the quicksands of time,
From the sonorous voices useless
To the deaf-mute winds of death,

I'll make you a land;
                    a pure plain
Where a mountain grows from glistening orchards,
In harmony, like a movement in a beautiful dream;

With one decisive breath, like a glass-blower
Who, before the fire, recalls a beauty
He has not learnt,
I'll make a refuge for the invulnerability
Which is your right.

2

I'll make a cool garden of light
For your shadow, just breaking into leaf,

The shadow I prise with my nails
From the mast of the years so it may never ripen
To empty black smoke,

I'll make a forbidden garden of light,
The transparent murmur of time.

3

I'll make you a pure season, with the voices
Of joyful waters fertile with sun,

A season with mornings of June rain
Whose birdsong glitters with bright metal
That will not rust,

A breathing-space for your blood, which absorbs
The golden years as bees are drawn to a poppy-field,
Drunkenly humming their barbed dream.

4

I'll make you a land where words turn of their own accord
Into birds, taking on lives of their own
That last as long as they have meaning,

A land which won't go away if you close your eyes,
Like a strip of light under someone else's door
Extinguished by a stranger's indifferent act;

With one decisive breath, like a trumpeter
Forced to transform his walls to black dust
And melt bitterly into the brass as if into death,
Suddenly over-ripe with impending miracle,

I'll make a refuge for your invulnerability:
A land where you cannot bury me.

Part IV

LOVE

For years I have been learning your features, where the days
Impress their tiny fires; for years I have memorised
Their shimmering uniqueness, and the latticed lightness
Of your movements behind the transparent draperies
Of the afternoon; and so I no longer recognise you
Outside the memory which surrenders you to me,
And every day I find it harder to tame the current of time
Which does not flow through you, through the gentle metal
Of your blood;
                    if you change, I change equally,
And with us that world built around an instant
Like fruit around a kernel, woven of unreal flesh
With the taste of lightning, the taste of dust, the taste of years,
The taste of snow melting on the flame of your skin.

For years I have known we are disappearing together;
You burnt through with the star of my memory, outside which
You steadily diminish, myself beautifully dispersed in you,
In every afternoon, in every room, in every day,
In everything which fills you slowly, like sand
Filling a riverbed;
                    and this, our moment,
Lasts longer than another's death.

WIND

Wind dressing and undressing the sea
In the torn lace of light, in a salty web,
Coarse between two embraces,

Wind sifting the pattern of tiny crystals
In the star of your iris,
Building a garden of rags in your eyes,

Wind giving your skin the colour
Of light, dry earth which bears a fruit tree
With pink-scented blossom,

Wind kindling the brief blaze of your hair
Which will consume my fingers
Like birds in a burning rye-field,

Wind the illusionist, wind the fire-eater,
Wind walking the tightrope of sleeplessness
Stretched from night to morning,

Wind flicking through time tonight like a dictionary,
Burying me in nouns of love
Light and bitter, like leaves of gleaming copper.

BIRD

I'm moulding a bird from a handful of air and fire,
A bird to burn more slowly
Than the fire inside you, the air around you,

A bird lighter than the pumice stone of wisdom,
To hover weightless in the dark layers
Of experience which force you to breathe,

A bird which will sing you a garden beyond the years,
By a sea of naked words where the wind
Draws circles unknown to Archimedes,

I'm moulding a bird from a handful of air and fire
To release it into your small, stormy sky
On the thin rein of my sleep,
On the thin rein of my blood.

PLACES WE LOVE

Places we love exist only through us,
Space destroyed is only illusion in the constancy of time,
Places we love we can never leave,
Places we love together, together, together,

And is this room really a room, or an embrace,
And what is beneath the window: a street or years?
And the window is only the imprint left by
The first rain we understood, returning endlessly,

And this wall does not define the room, but perhaps the night
Your son began to move in your sleeping blood,
A son like a butterfly of flame in your hall of mirrors,
The night you were frightened by your own light,

And this door leads into any afternoon
Which outlives it, forever peopled
With your casual movements, as you stepped,
Like fire into copper, into my only memory;

When you go, space closes over like water behind you,
Do not look back: there is nothing outside you,
Space is only time visible in a different way,
Places we love we can never leave.

LOVE IN JULY

1

Open this evening like a letter,
The writing smeared with the fine blood of birds
Consumed by the bright lava of midday,

Open this evening like a rose,
The dust, the copper, the sweat,
That constellation breathing on your skin,

Open this evening like a letter:
I'm hiding in the writing
Like a shadow in a cherry tree, motionless between the leaves,
Like midday in our blood,

Night is on the move, overgrown with rain,
With cherries, with the mutable diamonds of coolness –
Open this evening like a letter:

An illegible date, time without beginning,
And a legible signature –
                                        I love.

2

A taste of storm in the stem of the invisible rose
You absently twirl between your fingers;
A summer of black and gold,

But there is no wind, and the rain
Shimmers only on your words, like phosphor
On the seams of water;
A summer of black and gold,

And lightning, which travels more slowly than memory,
Will never shine upon us in the same place twice,

Lightning still heaped with flowers and snows,
Somewhere on its journey round the year –

A taste of rain on your lips,
A summer of black and gold.

WINTER LETTER

How strange you are when you're not here!
Between us, the air is choking on tiny flowers,
A snowstorm like a sweet disease. And when
My fingers touch you through the fence that rings
An ordinary dream, you seem about to speak
Of things I do not know: a wisdom
Gold between two words, like summer air
Between two islands. But it is easier for me
To reach you there than to imagine the space
Alleged to separate us (a night of violet salt,
A plain in whose silence I trace a straight line
Between the shrouded, starry woods –
A December night). Even if you're something else
Than all you know of yourself, such a night
As this, when the sea, frightened by snow,
Opens and flutters like an eye in my blood;
Even if you are strange, my love, here where you're not,
Lit like a flame – look – on the candle of your name
In the empty room of the spoken.

So many ways to make me
Depend on you all the more!

RAIN AFTER US

Rain after us, processions from a heavenly ocean
In a hissing pilgrimage over our land, my love,
Rain through the years, great constellations of drops
On the weightless branch of shadow growing after us,

Rain filling the print of your motion
In air still warm with my words, my love,
Everywhere I've loved you, at every position
Abandoned in battle, my gleaming shield;

Rain after us, the tremble of a wet bluebell
Where once was a word, but we have moved on,
Rain in gardens rising after us,
On the empty tracks, twin swords of flame –

But the mirrors grow dark with the weight of our images
Forever in love, in a place after us,
In the hissing of rain you no longer hear,
For you're listening to my voice.

V

THE ARGONAUTS

The sea let us be, engrossed with the eternity
In herself; and so we sailed, from shore
To shore, for days, for nights, for years.

The loveliest shores, of course, we left untouched:
Except for unravelled threads of scent borne on the wind
From the vast orchards at the ends of the earth,

Beyond the path of our sailing; and yet
We learnt love, and death, and a little sense,
Hard grains of gold in the sand of memory;

Yes, and the pride of adventure, defiled with blood
And washed in the clean winds, beneath the stars
Where we clumsily wrote our names.

We came back, in the end, to where we began;
The crew scattered like a necklace: our destiny's thread
Had snapped. The captain crushed beneath the keel.

The sea was still the same. Everything was still the same.
The ship, her ribs blossomed open, lies rotting on the starting
    shore,
But few know the secret:
                        the end does not matter,

What matters is only the sailing.

MARINE

My form, between this stone and a fruit
Ripened to flesh dark with the foam of a sun
Hemmed in between two similar flashes of death,

My form, a stranger to its source, most similar of all
To a sound clothed in the water I name:
Sea, fleshy shell of red fire;

My form, most similar of all to the dull green silver
Of the wind, etched with glittering images
And a heavy sun, bitter, hollow honeycomb

Buzzing with time beweaponed and winged;
My form, unrepeatable now, yesterday unremembered,
Tomorrow unknown, equally indestructible,

Bound to this sun with dark, salty threads of blood,
As battered ships are moored
To a yellow breakwater, between two voyages;

It won't open to a bullet, won't open to a knife,
And slips between your fingers, like water,
And when you squeeze the fruit, you hear the rustle of a tree,

You hear the roar of the sea.

SEPTEMBER

The year is hanging like a spider on a thread
In the forked smoke of pines, where the cones
Open like parasols, then turn to stone;

There, where the silence shimmers like a shoal of dead fish
Slaughtered last night with the sickle of the young moon,
A storm is climbing into the saddle, its spine bolt upright –

Look, a little flame peeled from the lips of the sea
Is reborn as a red leaf, and is singing,
Linked to the vine by a dark and bitter stem,

The fruit is swaying on the branch, the fruit in the woman's womb
On the salt waves of blood and the west wind:
The year is hanging like a spider on a thread.

BIRTH

Whose crimson voice pierced
His mother's leaf-thin time, already trembling
Like will-o'-the-wisp on a stem of water;

Who was frightened just now by the violent taste of air
Forcing the wet branches of lungs to burst into blossom;
Whose memory weighs less than lightning;

Who emerged from a wound
With an unscathed skin and a ravaged memory
Of a great garden of captive blood,
Of the light sometimes dreamt by the humbled;

Still sightlessly curled in the gesture of defence
With which he sank into his first sleep, as dense as coal,
As dense as the column of milk waking in his mother
Asleep in the pool of a smile,

(Behind a window the colour of a green star
One late autumn night, with dripping eaves,
And the rusty voices of birds through the fog,
And rocket launchers overgrown in constellations of dew):

My son, my blood blind and free again,
My son, my fear grown ripe to living flesh.

TYRRHENIAN SEA

Beyond olive trees grey with the ash
Of a night charred by the tracer-bullets of stars,
Beyond marshes rusty with grass, beyond leaning towers
And hills wet with the west wind –
The Tyrrhenian Sea,
                                a scented rag of blue
Torn apart by the thousand hooves of the sinewed air.

A flock of birds flies to meet us, a burst of buckshot
Peppering the rosy mortar on the low wall of morning;
In the fleshy leaves of figs ripens the bitterness
Of a rainy year, and the wind bears us the smell
Of dolphins axed to death on deck.

Towers lean over us carved in clouded ivory,
Towers dark with congealed blood, rinsed long
In the gentle acid of the rains, and on them settles a flame
Wafted by the wind from splintered shores;
Rivers strangled with sweet sand decompose in the plain,
Between the crickets and the smoke signals
Of the Etrurian pines; the sea rises and slowly unfurls
Like a flag.

And if only we could stay here
Between the word *rain* and the word *tree* and the word *star*,
In this plain, between the hills, if only –

But you are already a little older, my love,
And this menacing world betrays us
And so keeps its balance,
                                one more day.

INVENTORY OF MOONLIGHT

An Istrian moon
Stained with salt and the west wind,
Over the lean and dark green slopes
Gnawed by the were-air of equinox,

A moon which might have been a match
Struck on the stairs of a Belgrade house
Razed to the ground sixteen years before,

A house razed to the ground sixteen years before,
Tenanted now by tainted fires and children
Turned to angels in accordance with the stories,

An angel, a smile emerging from the ashes
Like a leaf from a tree, defenceless;
An angel rehearsing a gesture on his wall
For centuries, with unknown intent,

The gesture I make in sleep to ward off the birds
Liming the wet cordite and singing like machine-guns
When, drenched in sweat, I want to wake in a garden,

A garden turned in compassion towards the sea
And steeped in the blue anaesthetic of afternoon shadows;
The old lace of light, yellowing and frayed,
And the sea's fire between the trees,

A tree in the wind, half fire already,
A tree which seems to resemble the name
I've long been inventing for you, my love, in vain –

In a razed house, in the dust, the wind,
In the years, the fire, the gardens,
Yesterday, today, and tonight,
Lit like a match:

In the gnawing air of equinox
Over the lean and dark green slopes,
Stained with salt and the west wind,
An Istrian moon.

A PERFECT AUTUMN

Sea without spray, a perfect autumn leaning
Beautiful over serenity's abyss,
A crystal of concentrated flame, the flesh
Of fruit, of crumbling soil which soaks up the rain;
And death which again can only be a proof
Of a beauty which is weaker than itself.

Check every cartridge of this awareness, which
Is about to fire upon its own genesis:
The false bullet kills. No motive is needed
For gardens, though death will surely find one.
But death again can be no more than a proof
Of a beauty which is weaker than itself.

This hour in the ripened resin of amber
Is drenched to the core with a denser balance,
Is drunk, like the vine, with its own sweetness,
And cannot support the form of its splendour;
And death again can be no more than a proof
Of a beauty which is weaker than itself.

The stars are forever slower than the night
When air is bewitched to the were-form of wind,
And lovers forever slower than the blood
Which gradually fills them with future ashes,
And every death can be no more than a proof
Of a beauty which is weaker than itself.

Check every bullet of this silence sniping
Down at you from out of memory. Feel the flash
Of the lightning, the texture of the bullet's
Whine, so that you may realise: yes, it was good.
For every death has been no more than a proof
Of a beauty which was weaker than itself.

Those who remember have a more beautiful
Fading. This autumn is already crumbling
Because it is perfect; but beyond hearing
Appears a bird, beyond sight the stars begin.
And every death can be no more than a proof
Of a beauty which is weaker than itself.

ROMAN QUARTET

I

Spring: the Piazza Navona trembles like a ship
Tacking towards a tested star, in a southerly wind,
Age-old, malarial and sweet.
                       Here I eavesdrop
Night after night on the stronger one inside me,
Comparing his heated voice, fogged by the breath of blood,
With the winged, haphazard words dressed in the voices
Of late lovers on the benches, this night of blind travellers
On the ship of my pride, sailing to the schedule of my death;
It was only this afternoon (after a shower of warm rain,
On the balustrade of that stairway ravaged by the fires of tiny
Flowers, above the roofs overgrown with gardens, with fruit,
With smoke and lemon-coloured light) that I believed
In you again, familiar, virgin world;
                          then night came,
Serene, inhuman, filled with the ultimate fantasy of fire
And bursting with another eternity, and overtook me
On the square in a fever of wind, a roaring of waters,
Listening in to the irresistible force which lifts me

From my blood like a wave, sets me sparkling,
Then scatters me asunder.
                              Yes, these relentless nights
Gouged by the stems of exploded stars,
Announced in the shattered tongues of fountains,
Strong on the black-green slopes of solemn pine,
Nights forever too big, overcrowded
With years of unknown intent; the strongest nights
Cause me to vanish all the faster, like a flame
Fed with the heady milk of the feral air, proud to assert itself,
Condemned not to recognise itself
In times of fire and wind.

II

Mornings in the Via Statilia, as the wet, glittering voices
Of birds in the garden opposite, already peeled bare,
Enter through the window like bullets of gentleness;
Still, phosphor mornings of love,

As the room blossoms into a hall of mirrors
Duplicating a single movement, or maybe the colour
Of a dress on a chair;
                           whence this transformation of dream
Into the image of a world which exists, gentle, just for us,
Until we have set within it, like bright castings,
And morning falls away like a die, already cracked?

See – by day we are complete; or so we seem,
Like a statue voiceless until you smash it
And waken with fire the void and stars inside,
Scattering a recognised form proclaimed as purpose.
And this is your day:
                           these streets that glitter,
Accepting your footsteps like fate, fountains shot through
With sun, an espresso beneath the already dusty leaves
At an absurdly tiny table, a conversation about that star
On the Greek madonna's shoulder, and your smile which I kept
From the steps, between the blossom and the barbarous
Clicking of cameras (*Say, Helen, what is this place?*);

I remember shop windows releasing your shadow
Like a leaf of copper and water; but where were you?
Perhaps you still lingered somewhere in the morning, or had fallen
Asleep at the first bullet of waking, which cannot quite kill
Your true face of fire,
                              my love.

III

That garden on the Aventine, before us and after the rain,
Brimful with air, laid waste by the beauty of the years,
Surely we'd been here before?
                              There were gates of glass
You smashed with your smile, oblivious,
Happy and tired with walking; then water splashed
In a fountain, wet wings fluttered away, something rustled
In the cool, bristling pines. This garden existed,
Drawn with a sure hand on the map of time, beautiful
Before a sky the colour of morning sea-water (even
Though it was afternoon, and the city all round us
Was peeling leaves of sun from its domes to expose
Its centuries, intimately, sluttishly, like the wet
Washing and gutted birds on the Campo dei Fiori:
A city effortlessly present, from one instant to the next).
And yet we couldn't quite believe this garden
Was real; it was all too close, too tailor-made
For us, and might all fall apart
At a word, a sudden move.
                              Even today I have my doubts
About that garden (as the wind might doubt its name, the sea
Its taste), that garden slowly receding
And already starting to glimmer like a constellation
Orbiting a mythical year; a garden like a word
Spoken in love, and wafted away on the wind; a garden
On the Aventine, after us, and before an unknown rain.

IV

It's time you were asleep, unknown lovers,
Whose faces night is tapping away at like a goldsmith,
Fashioning with a little fire a beauty he will forget.
Let this square, with its three fountains, be empty:
Air will knit together over the space of your bodies,
As painlessly as lichen, as water. And don't look back:
All you know you hold inside you.
                              And a strong night
Is coming like the sea, with no explanation or love.
It's time you were asleep, unknown lovers: woe betide
Those who stay awake, chained to the gates of the gardens
Of fire, as they used to chain tactless prophets.

It's time you were asleep, so you may not see
Your shortened shadows, so you may teach your blood
Obedience. See: one by one, the windows are burning out;
Behind them, the certainty of objects you love:
Lamp, bed, wall.
                  And a strong night
Is coming like the sea, with no explanation or love.

Inhuman city, butchered beauty of duration, with velvet
Moths fluttering from your wounds, with swallows
Swarming at the intersections of your veins, city of wonders –
I will stay on alone, to see you renounce sleep, to see
A strong night, by which I vanish even faster,
Grow bitter with your name.
                        For there are places
Of last-ditch defence: sentries raise their voices
Like weapons, and are dust; water and wind
Dismantle the glistening flesh of lovers; and yet
A star which returns must recognise something,
Or else it would not return.

THE SEA AFTER RAIN

Now I know this flash, once again, at last, this
Still and limpid furrow of ocean, sown with
Short-lived fire, the years I remember, with the
Seeds of transition,

This astringent evergreen, this unleavened
Earth in which a knife will not rust, a bone not
Rot, this sudden, coppery taste of thunder
On heaven's palate,

And this climate, full of substantial splendour,
Where the trees are dusky, the shadows bright, this
Flesh of summer skilfully coaxed to ripeness,
Azure and gold, its

Fibres threads of memory, threads of fire, I
Recognise this flesh, once again, at last, these
Foam-fields, flower-patterned migrations on the
Skin of the breezes,

Close to death, but closer to pride, a pride in
Being sole and rightful possessor of this
Blood of mine, this thin and excited blood so
Bitter with summer,

Of my skin, still riddled with terror's bullets,
Branded by the sparks of another's death, of
This my spine, the root of a shadow lighter
Yet than a bullet,

Now I feel that I can recall, again, at
Last, the art of dignity, scattered phrases,
As the shafts of images strafe me, searing
Salvos of sunlight,

Now, again, I know I can lay a bitter
Claim to all this sea which is rinsed with summer

Rain, I know a thread of undying fire runs
Right the way through me,

Now I know I am the decisive, chosen
One within the presence of stone, of birds, of
Trees, though small I be in this blaze, and lost like
Words in a whirlwind,

For I can remember a time outside me,
I, already scathed by decay, just like this
Summer, match my blood to the rain of light, one
Sea to another,

For I can remember, intoxicated
With escape from silence's traps, still set to
Snap at my thin speech, at the rites of blood more
Lasting than I am,

Wholly of this world, like this day which lingers
Still disguised in scents of the scudding showers,
All imprinted into the sinewed air, this
Afternoon's ozone,

Now I know this flash, once again, at last, I
Proudly weep at last, though I shed no tears, I
Match my weight at last to the weight of sea, to
Equal my freedom,

To this world I give back the black stars clustered
In my blood, I give back the clouded ice of
Fear, the taste of earth from my mouth, perhaps a
Freshly-cast bullet,

To this world I give back my death's down-payment,
And the bitter root of my sight's defeat, the
Murky spray of oaths in my ear's thin shell, a
Hades of weeping,

Part V

To this world I give back the right to count for
Nothing in the eyes of the sea, the hearing
Of the wind, I give back my blood's black stars, the
Mead of abasement,

Though so small, so lost in this blaze of crimson
Silver, in this ocean of salty fire, one
Afternoon high over a rain-rinsed sea, my
Flame is still glinting.

PROLEGOMENA TO WAKING: SHORES

1

For water's imagination to take the shape of a beast,
For wind to learn its first word,
For light to thicken, conceiving a bird
In its own image,

For the sea to feel it is,
For the sea to say freedom,
Its teeth needed breaking,
It needed naming;

Hence the creation of shores.

2

Whether you sang of coasts, sketched shorelines
In memory, in pride,
On your imprecise charts where flies
Foul the roses of winds,

The shores know nothing of it all;
They just exist

(Awake, you might say,
But older than sleep),
Heedless of all

But the nutritious decay
Of the seasons, the scattering of fire
Begotten with them
Like flesh on the bone –

Remembering this, they sense what they are.

3

Threshold of an ocean's consciousness,
Shores of morning copper, of fruit
Which tastes of the burnt-out blood
Of reiterated years,

Dark magnetic coasts, eroded
By the green lichen of fertility,
Plaster coasts, undermined
By the blue needles of the tide,

Shores pulled in every direction
By the points of dividers, patterned,
Helpful if need be,

See: shores all round us,
Strong signs of land.

4

A space which reflects upon itself
Notes its own vacillation,
Draws a decisive border –

Only then can the growth
Of hesitant voices begin, can the seed
Inhale air and flame,

Only then can an eye open one day
To the sight of a gentle sea
Reaping its blue
With sickles of light.

5

Summer begins, and somewhere a landslide of air
Shifts the cries of the birds,

Shores glisten before the rain.

6

Then come the masons
With dust in their lashes, their hands
Braced against time,

Then come the masons
With their chisels, their dignity, their brief blood,
Then come the masons

To cut free the stone, discover a form
More swiftly than wind or water,
To move a year, a word,

To carve, with burning eyes.

7

There's fire inside you, quarries,
And the dense coolness of the vanished shadows
Of those whose name is also mine;

Quarries salty on the shores,
Like small wounds opened with the teeth
Of golden leeches;

(But we form the stone into a mighty spine
To make our duration grow tall.)

Yet the battle is fought in an eternal circle:
We break up a shore
To build a wall.

8

But they say the most beautiful shores,
Swelling on a pure sea
And heavy with orchards, foaming
With starry flowers, with chlorophyll
And benign silence,

They say the most beautiful shores
Mentioned in reliable songs
Have a gentle climate
And so forth;

Those unknown shores
Which, if they did not exist,
Would need inventing.

9

Shores before every sea,
The only frontier,

And all the birds, joined with reins
Of invisible blood: were they to fly free,
They would not be birds;

Shores as reliable as our most recent tears;
And our golden shadows
And our bones and chisels
In their rinsed-out wrinkles;

There is no beginning, no end:
Only shores.

10

For the sea to bleed about itself,
For the wind to learn its name,
For the eye to open,

For the seed to inhale flame,
For the blood to become a hand,
For the hand to lift the chisel,

For the light to feel a bird
Move in its womb, and smile –

See: shores all round us,
The stern features of earth.

VI

ALGOL

1

The water I remember: a leaf
Trembling like a hand on a horse's bare back;
A stream which set diadems between its reeds,
Now cocooned in memory,
                              a wet butterfly
With two dark vowels for wings,

Or the water of sweat, or damp which opens upon the wall
The pallid landscape of a rainy summer
With trees of spongy fog,

Water in gentle hollows, like the evening sky,
Where the first salt crystals form
Along invisible matrices of light,

And last of all, the water in my mother's milk, her blood –
Surely all I hoard in precious nouns,
In the silence after each defeat,
Surely this whole wealth of wetness
Cannot all cruelly evaporate,
Cannot be consumed, ashless,
In a single, sudden flash,
                              arrested
Like a bird before an unknown lens,
Pressed like a stain
Into the bitter skin of some unknown sea?

The water I remember,
And all the voices
Glittering with dew like the metal of morning bridges?

2

I remember that star
Clouded as the ruby glass of old goblets,
That star, toxic word eating away at texts

Written in windy towers,
I remember the unsteady glint above the ships
With an abandoned diary, one night without wind,
On a flat calm of Indian ink (so many possibilities,
But not a single legible sign!),

I remember that star unleafing like a butterfly,
The shimmer dispersing like hyperite,
The mild leprosy of the September sky,
I remember that star girdled with a web of equations,
The star which reminded me to feed a hope
As the whine of a bullet reminds one of an embrace,

And that star's explosion,
Which sets no gnomons trembling on their dials
As they rust in the old, wet gardens of this planet
Which I can pronounce,
That sign legible in a perfect night sky,
That light clothed in the false flesh of years
Will also interpret me,
                    my fear,
And the tiny vampires I'm poisoning
With the sweet pride of my daily blood.

        3

Great, rainy summers,
Trees bright with a burly glitter,
And our ruined excursions, my love,
Somewhere in a space which still thrills us
With its unrealised image:
                        a lake polished
Like marble, ornate with veins of light,
A clearing heaped with ozone between two rains,
A safe afternoon, shingled roofs
Rinsed and dried to the patina of old silver;

And then the brief nights, which we remember
Fleshed on the frail skeleton of lightning
As we name each other, as if for the first time,

Beneath a window overgrown with shivering scales,

Or the showers at night on the open street
With the naked voice of a bird
And chestnut leaves as heavy as nursing breasts:

Rainy summers, beautiful stains in the rooms of the years,
Winds weighed down with raindrops,
If we don't manage to wish you farewell,
If we don't manage to wish you farewell . . .

4

I remember water, recall a star
Whose name I am afraid to say,

A star which could drink this world's water dry
In the delirium of an inconceivable thirst,
A star which this word cannot hold;

And all my words
Sling-shot into windy orbits
About an inconstant space in which I have squeezed
Love, and rebellion, and memory,
As the sea imprints its fires
On the seasons of the shores,

All my words, my speech,
My knife beneath the pillow, the glass of water on the table,
Images bartered for the right to pronounce them,
Names I slip as a bribe to time,
And birds I ring with the fragile silver of memory,

All this might weaken
At the imposed moment of decision –

And so a star reminds me of silence,
A star shines over my book before I sleep.

SNOWY NIGHT

Snowy night, onslaught of white purity, snowy night
Of the cold roe of sterile stars, but
So quick to catch fire:
                          in the violet branches
The treacherous substance of time, hidden and terrible,
In the bird's feather, in the blizzard. Snowy night,
But ever fewer words for the final defence,
For resistance to a glorious roar of absurdity –

And I already suspect the word bird, it might fly away,
Suspect the word water, it might evaporate,
Suspect the word wind, the word star, the word rain,
The word death, with its all too lifelike gleam;

Ever fewer words, precious few, perhaps,
For the moment of decision:
                          perhaps just two or three,
Enormous, lost beforehand, erect
In the burning air – the only poem.

Will they suffice, wide world, my pyrrhic victory,
For me to protect you, for me to defend you,
Extend you till the moment of truth?

Snowy night, flowers of white sulphur,
Foam on a wave of fire.

MARCH

Snow-covered hills suddenly all around us,
Icebergs in the light-blue sea of afternoon
Bristling with leafless woods, white magnets
Fuzzy with needles –
                tell me, where are we?
I remember a similar pattern of excitement
On a similar afternoon, scarcely ruffled
From within (like a pond filled with an aspic light
Seeping from a drowned, still-moving rose of sun);

Something, sweet current of years, is repeating itself,
Something unreasoned but kind,
Like a mother's unthinking kiss, like a phosphor word
Invented, forgotten and found in love,

Or my weeping, a boy's weeping, repeated in the swan
Beating its wings again and again on the edge
Of the frozen pond, then smudged into the spell
Of the afternoon sun –
                and snow-covered hills,

Hills whose names I do not know, for they are beautiful and strange
In the ozone's invisible blaze, in their slow shift
Away from today, this horror, these words.

SPRING LITURGY FOR A DEAD POET

to Branko Miljković

1

Are you alone at last? Alone enough
To say to the earth: here is another name
For memory, for taste, for the despair which
Fills you when spring insists that you become a
Miracle, for all within you transformed to
An echo beneath a fallen arch of blood?
Alone enough at last to smile at the fire
Of an uncatalogued star, in orbit still
About the self-same centre, where you stood just
A day ago, but where silence stands today?
Because you wanted to be alone, heavy
With the crucial moment, to be alone for
A night in whose course your blood mingled with time
Like two swift waters;

Are you alone at last? Alone enough
To be proof against any beauty? Or does
The taste of reddish clay already remind
You of a summer, a mine of radiance,
And do you already recognise the air
Above you, brimful of scattered signs, of words
Descending on you like a pitiless grace
And stripping the brief peace from your eyebrows? See –
Death is outside the resolution.
                                        In vain
Do you summon your angel with a silence
Upright as a falconer's cry: for every
Question is the same, and the sea still roars through
All the seasons of the year, and the fires still
Flow the same way down.

Now it is time
For you to move on. All the voices in the
World are stretching upright in your hearing, are

Trembling upon their long stems. And the wind will
Turn the page, so we may repeat after you:
When a poet dies, he furnishes a proof
That the bird still flies, that death does not exist.

3

Do not mourn this disarmed voice of mine today,
Unable to halt this spring with words; now I know
This spring has existed since time out of mind, that tomorrow's
Rain is already filling the lake of this morning's hearing.
And the flight of yesterday's bird brings me news
Of every deluge, of every leaf-tipped twig.

If this be a dream, let no one wake me;
Scattered like sparks in the wind, now I can dream myself,
And the air you breathe, already steeped in summer,
Bears, like an ancient veil, the image of my face,
And somewhere all my dreaming is ended
In motion, shadow, rebellion, hills.

Your faces, my friends, are fading from memory.
Your words are fading, and the positions of your voices
On the empty fields of the game. Yet everything still remains
The same distance away: star and flower and tree,
Wind and season. And the ocean that greets you
When you see it, remains my ocean still.

Maybe this is the way to remember beauty,
To shape a poem, to dream a word;
See, the flight of yesterday's bird brings me news
Of every deluge, of every leaf-tipped twig;
Leave me to dream, to doubt, to burn away:
Do not mourn this disarmed voice of mine.

THE SINGER AND THE KING

It is for you to be stronger; my fate
Is to endure one song more,
This fire I gird seven times about my loins,

And to look into your eyes which always squint a little,
Eyes in which wrath shimmers and cools
Like unstable metal
In the windy courtyards of your foundries,

And to avoid you constantly, as rain skirts a desert;
But we are both enchanted: you stronger,
                                        I more conscious of myself,
And the game goes on, in every song,

In every song where you thirstily recognise roses
And the gold leaf of vowels,
And I my death –

Always, when in the space between two words
An empire awakes, unknown,
Suddenly disturbed, under arms, like an ant-hill
Awakened by a stray spark.

In the end, my King, we are both powerless:
In the song which links us there rises a sky
And a perilous land peopled without us,

And every night the known stars are a little farther.

YOUNG WOMAN FROM POMPEII

I curled up, shrinking like the pupil of an eye
Adapting too late to that cruel glare,
And fallen to earth, I rested my burnt forehead
On my arm.
         After that
My name disintegrated even faster
Than my tender flesh, in suffocating bitterness.
I forgot to count, to breathe,
And to look back. I was emptiness,
I was the dark cloud of my movement,
A bubble in a sea of dead fire. Thus
I awaited the slimy touch of wet clay
Filling me without passion, as water
Fills a footprint on deserted sands.

And what do you know of me now? Barely something
Of my brief wish to outlive myself,
Only a gesture, perhaps of weeping, and a shape
Sealed accidentally and in haste.
So how can I tell you that there exists
A domain where I am more real than the voice
Trying to imprison me, more solid
Than the light in which you look at me?
You think you know me? Go on,
Touch this shoulder: I am not there.
But my touch is much lighter:
                  there –
You are not who you were a moment ago. I know you
And burn on your shoulder, before the fire,
Before the ashes, before and after everything.

MARINE II

Let us stay a while
In this silence before a pure wrath
Which will not break since it is already within us
Like lightning in the bitter blood of sea, like a wild seed
In the red dust I spit upon to knead into a god,
Into a wild rose, the dream of a searing bee
With a sterile sting of diamond,

In this silence on the shore,
This recollection whose echo permeates the stone from within
Like sweat, here where foam-blossom shivers
On the edge of flotsam, sleep on the sea's lashes
Heavy with salt for all the wounds of the world;

Look, a bird's skeleton still bewitched with the symmetry of flight,
Empty tin cans, metal embroidered with roses of rust
Like a thin veil with blood from a face –

Just a few scattered signs
And our voices mingling like blood,
Like the smells of lovers, like history;

Rebel words which emerge like stars
At the right, the predicted point.

BELGRADE AIRPORT, JUNE

A young beast surfaces from the haze,
Slender metal muscles in a blaze of blue,
Sound condensed through a clouded lens, fire out loud,

And on the terrace a few flowers, a little wind, unease
Like a harness-bell in the ringing glasses, where ice
Painlessly loses its sharp, transparent edges, like a word
Disarmed in the sweetness of use;

Look, down it comes,

And I'll tell you again –
        travellers live in illusion,
Nothing happened while they were dreaming
Under the anaesthetic of the upper abyss, distorted
In the concave chalice of afternoon, riders
Of the arrow's shadow:

Their imprecise measure defines everything still,

And the beast breathes on the clean runway, as if after a love
Which has no consequences.

ORPHEUS' SECOND DESCENT

Descending a wordless road, his voice effaced,
Empty-handed in this penultimate act,
Descending, a bitter fire girdling his waist,
To the flapping of black bats whose bites are chased
Into his claylike flesh, all gaping and cracked.

Spring's wet constellations wheel sodden and slow,
Rootlets smoulder like fuses under the glades,
The house of silver sifts full of drifting snow,
Its mirrors cloud over, roses bud and blow,
A youthful lightning wakens to hone its blades;

119

Orpheus shines down tunnels pitch-black and warm,
Lord of his own domain of violet night,
Without a guide, without a task to perform,
In his body's caverns rebel flowers swarm:
A phosphorescent leper with scabs of light.

He recognises time and place, every sign
A witness to distant defeat, sees the print
Of the scream, and walks on; the fire of a vine
Breaks into leaf behind him, and like a mine
Of wakened images, the hollow shadows glint.

Downwards, free of the weight of promises, free
Of pledges and rules of play, no end in sight;
Every step strikes root; but branchless is this tree,
Weird, self-dreaming, forever striving to see
The source of its glory through the depths of night.

Like tracer fire, his every footstep strikes a spark;
Left with a single memory, leprous, on
He walks, away from his end, back in an arc
To his starting-point; as seeds gleam through the dark,
Ancestral depths: a death and a love long gone.

The summers sing like sirens, but on he goes,
Orpheus in the tunnel, bitter and dumb;
Close your eyes; and when you are roused by the throes
Of pullulating blood, by a spindrift rose,
Then in your ears his road, his footsteps will drum.

NEREID

1

One afternoon, after the wind, after the vengeance,
After the voices and fever on the evergreen tide,
I thought you were not there –
But you lay half-choked in silence,
In your sated, invisible blood; scorching,
Battered, with golden lice in your hair;

You change too quickly
For me to learn to love you with these words, this noose,
This passion as imprecise as a sundial
In the damp garden of a northern year.

2

Flowers of salt in your sweaty armpit,
The inconceivable give of stone
Barrenly heated in the midday sun,
And a butterfly, two symmetrical flames
Flickering on a compass needle lighter than air –
A more reliable guide around
Your defences, the obliviousness
Beneath your mask of peeling gold leaf,

To reach your name turned in sleep, in smell,
Like a long-lost key in a keyhole.

3

In the motionless air the limestone wing
Flakes as far as the curdled glint
Of a sea of engine oil, emerald and glass;

I cannot know all that you might do,
So open to every moment,
Machine invented to rust and build yourself,
You whose wet and starry shrewdness challenges me

To cast a stone, addressing you in your own tongue –
But you change again,
                                  and the imprecise word is already dispersing
Like the brief rose of foam after the stone.

4

Crystalline scabs grow in your shallow wounds
Like silt at the bottom of unwashed shells;
You wake with the itching of salty diamonds
When the voices of crickets fall silent
In the constellations of cones, poisoned
By the pale blue shadows, as if by cyanide fumes.

You wake refreshed, move roses of flesh
Electrified at the turn of the tide, like an orchard waking to rain
When the first droplet taps a single blossom –

And are ready to go on with a game won before it began.

5

The night you are brushed by lightning, purer
Even than you, than the milky horror
Soon to silt up the mirrors of your blood,

The horror which feeds the huge, luminous sea-urchins
Huddled in the pines above your sleeplessness,

The night you are brushed by lightning, just to
Remind you of the terrible balance which rules
You too, beauty with bitter palates of pearl

Open by morning as blossom, as splinters
Whetted with stubborn gentleness, spattered with used foam.

6

He who takes you without love in the blizzard
Of your sparks, living water, shore unto yourself,
Water lit from within like a church,

He who takes you without love, like the wind which strips
The tear-dust and graven gold from your skin,
He who takes you without love

Will go blind to the vital details,
To tomorrow's fallen stone, to the silence which reigns
As your poison's gleaming tide nears its full –

When he turns, it will be too late.

7

You seem so peaceful as you arrange your mirrors,
Snares of light; but the chase remains invisible,
Concealed by your delay in reflecting
The effortless flight of a bird, the fall of a cone,

You seem so peaceful between your rocks
Which turn the air all salty
As the touch of metal darkens water.

You seem so peaceful before each death,
Encircled by the shadows of boats
On an open sea of copper soldered with cold water.

8

Look, it's autumn, and you're getting drenched in your
Flimsy chasuble of wet sparks, between the pine trees
Dipped in morning silver;

Winter is coming, wind is stretching at the ropes,
You will be all alone with the explosions of an empty sea
In your chambers of light,
Smiling, so sure of yourself –

These words of mine recognise you, words
Stoned in the whirl of your flowery shingle
Far, far away.

VII

Kalemegdan

KALEMEGDAN

1

Lightning tree, forked, unique,
Shivering in the pouring rain, your weightless fruit
Ripe in an instant,

Lightning tree, a bird was singing in your branches,
Singing a harsh wisdom, already ripped apart
By the next split second,

And its song, multiplied on every side
In the sulphur and silver of vast trees
As if in mirrors,

The song of the bird in your leaves, lightning tree,
Over the rivers' scalding waters, over the ridge
Where breathes a ravaged fortress, and rain-wet
Lovers speak the world,

The song of your bird, lightning tree,
The song of your bird, weightless fruit-tree of flame,
Said:
  there is hope, just check
How far you are from me,
From the garden I hear in your blood;
And the ground you stand on is mine –

Lightning tree, pure in the pouring rain.

2

And the world could start right here –
From this nexus of fire, this lump of red
Dug from the air as if from an unhealed
Wound, O septic history,
From this point I plot by stars
The colour of bullets, the colour of love,

And enter upon a map without a scale;
I print the austere, floral ideogram on my skin
With a kiss, sketch it in the wind: a rose
Of blazing air,

And say: here I cease to remember,
Here I am, since the beginning and at the end,
Like a seeing stone set in a fiery ring,
A pure circle, my only measure,

Here on this headland
Where the air makes cruel love
And, after the passion, kills all witnesses –

A word circled by a whirl of voices,
A copper queen in a bitter, deserted hive of light:
The world could start right here.

3

But the world is finished, long before this star
Choked in its own blood, slowly clotting to ivy
But vaporising and catching flame at the touch of summer,

Long before this star, stirring
Like a hornets' nest of winds, like a refuse tip,
Like a fortress with lovers along the bastion wall
And lead roses set in alveoli of stone,

Before what never stops being
A star, granary of fire,
And the shattered syllables of years
Hard to pronounce;

A world always finished before the finest of chances,
Sang the bird,
                or perhaps I merely remembered it
Above these rivers since time out of mind,

In this star, this citadel,
Here on these burning stairs.

4

Firm indications, stubborn roses in an ocean of ashes,
Flame which seals a charter,
Air filled with writing, water's seal broken,
A cruel script, a forbidden tongue. –

My coming or yours, my love,
Never on time, but never too late:
Will it suffice? But meanwhile a cruel
Rose holds court –

Firm indications, but why? These rivers
Fuse out loud, like two metals,
These rivers are always the same, these trains of barges
Laden with last night's rain, with munitions,
Wheel in a burst of fire, camouflaged grain-boats
Or ships of stars.

– And yet, sang the bird – and yet,
Just recognise, and then you'll know the reason why:
The seals are still unbroken, so every decree still holds,
Though the rest you'll have to invent. This, in the end,
Is why you are here.
                        Bird, I recognise full well
That I am this cruelty's witness,
And this is why I sing.

5

All my dead in this wind,
The fourth night now, the fifth night now,
The window like the whipped eye of a horse,

All my dead in this wind,
With the leaves, the dust, the years,

And my mouth full of blood and tenderness,
My tongue pierced with the golden pin
My mother once tried to find in her sleep,

The fourth night now, the fifth night now,
Wind around the house, pure dry flame,

Afloat on insomnia lighter than air,
I say their names,
Defend a world I did not create,

I justify myself, therefore I am.

6

But here, alive between the living, confident between the dead,
I find, flame, my most beautiful justification.
                                    The keepers
Of the seals, if they came back, would be unable
To tell us apart – the keepers, who left once and for all
When the misunderstanding first began,
Flags flying, weapons shouldered,
Down the clear slope, down a morning
Where, blossom-like, the first scents of blood were unfolding.

I justify myself in this morning, in my name,
Here where my coordinates cross, in sea-coloured ink
With which I write down names, in order to make them
Mine, to stave off a defeat impossible
As long as there's something to justify,

Alive between the living, present between the dead
On every firing ground where battle breathes,
Where a wave rises, breaks and retreats,
In every position, upon this ridge,
Hideously armed, though unasked,
And my name explodes! But what does it matter:
The wind blows back the syllables, a little gold, an echo –

And this is my justification.

7

But lovers find a simpler justification
Whilst they are together, heedless double stars
In the brief infinity of their orbit, in the rain,
In the constellations of a wet summer, in the wind
Beneath the bristling trees on the glacis,
                                        happy
On the green keel of the ravelin, above the scarps
Of a fortress they do not notice;
                                        preoccupied,
They think they are stronger. Their justice glitters
To meet a great sea of blood, like a pier;
They know this, and this is their reason: to grow bigger
For an instant, for the wing-flick of an angel they make
Of earth, of blossom, of breath, of light, of sweat;

– Only one thing is missing: to make their peace
With me, sang the bird;
                                but the lovers heard nothing,
For their time has blossomed into years,
And their hearing is beautifully ruined
With colour, like chlorophyll in autumn gardens.

8

Between a citadel and a garden: how many chances,
How much blood for the wind, in its Cyclopean indecision,
To rip out loud like a wet silk flag,
How many undrawn parallels, how many
Shouts from the towers, how many towers melted like wax
In the passion of air, how much passion
In repeating a sentence: the world could start right here,
How many petals on the wet skin of lovers,

How many ways of stating: never on time,
But never too late, how many delays
In the passage of barges, the exploding of a unrealised
Year, the breath of a bullet, a word,

How many chances in the garden, in the citadel,
Amongst the dead and the lovers, who recognise each other
With brief touches, like the blind, like conspirators,
How many chances to start a world

Already finished, star, already finished, geometry,
Already finished, great trees on the bastion wall,
Finished long before this chance, never on time
But never too late.

9

It's one thing to be finished, flame, but another
To state your finality,
                              as does the sea,
Starting again at every instant, immature,
Polisher of inconstant diamonds, eternal beginner,
Sea perfect from constant beginning, finished
Since time out of mind. It's one thing to be finished,

Another to endure. Rain evaporates from bronze
Peopled with voices, from leaves, from weapons,
From red brick, from the Danube's tarnished silver,
As the rain splashes down. The same rain.
The flesh of history rots around a star, a city rises
In the same air, the same dusty light,
The same rain which tastes of saltpetre and roses,
And the Twins, full with the same inflammable milk,
Softly go on with their game.
                              This,
In the end, is how to endure:
I recognise death in order to feed her a rose
In a meantime which is mine for free
By reason of my coming, by reason of my presence
In a citadel, a garden, this flesh, this quicklime of stars,
In these words.

10

Lightning tree, pure in the fertile, pouring rain,
Weightless fruit-tree of fire, home to a nightingale
Already consumed, already formed, already doomed,

Lightning tree, vein in the hardest marble,

I can always return to your shade,
Lightning tree, forked, unique.

VIII

A BITTER SUMMER'S FIRES STILL WHEEL

A bitter summer's fires still wheel
To turn in winter's fiery reel
As winds from sodden roses peel.

The compass needle spins around
In frantic search for signs unfound,
In death's own field her songs resound.

What must I say now to this bone,
Which is too weak to bridge alone
This gulf of spite, its depths unknown?

Where is the word which will unite
My end, its blackness flaring bright,
With glimmers of a stronger light?

A starry graveyard, maggot spawn,
Teems golden through the dregs of dawn,
In rotting flesh the bees now swarm.

A bitter summer's fires still wheel
And ever tighter hubwards reel,
Our shadows longer on each heel.

Tree of lightning, white-veined pillar,
Blazing feathers, songbirds' killer,
Teste David cum Sibylla.

When round the wet winds fire laps,
And when the compass needle snaps,
And when the sea vacates the maps,

Then through our lips shall blood, so lame,
Spit out at last the perfect name
And thicken to the mead of shame?

I sing the fruit, my faith I swear
In fruit which dreams up water, air,
For freedom is the bond they bear;

Each opportunity so thin,
Defeat of lines once straight I sing
Defeat in nested spheres that spin,

I sing my faith unto this bone,
Unto this word, which will be known
To endless wordlessness alone.

CYPRESS IN POČITELJ

Clear hour-hand of the sun, slow green shadow
Of everlasting noon;
      carved stone crumbles
All round in its own time, far removed
From this growing, this candle's body
Built through burning, inserting its
Invisible flame into the thirsty fibres of air
Where it slowly darkens, flickering still –

Salmon-twitch in the river, and wind entangled
In a creeper; a stone breaks free from the tower
And falls with a forked echo. Midday.

A unit of forgotten measure
Slowly outgrows itself;
      the cypress rises,
Quivering in the sun, gold-green, upright;
Careful marker of a star among stars.

PLATEAU

That plateau in the spasms of spring wind,
Floating low beneath a star still wet with snows
Whose tender flesh was feeding subterranean swarms of daffodils,

A plateau black with bristling pines, dreaming ozone
On the snake-lips of lightning and singing in their sleep,
Great, bitter anemones of an upper ocean,

When I say to my friends – leave me alone:
Look, I'm no stranger here – and lay speech aside
Like a weapon-heavy belt in the wet grass:
The wind's fingers on my shoulder recognise the joint,
The forgotten motion of a boy hurling a stone,
Clumsily and unerringly, between the self-same stars;

Leave me alone – the house was very close,
I recall the spot, scorched into every map,
There the wind whirls around the years, there the wind
Weds the voice of a young woman singing her son to sleep,
Weds it with a ring of black gold; leave me alone –
Look, the stone returns, the woman smiles, goes over to the
    window
And says: a star just fell –
                    when I say to my friends . . .

That plateau, in a fever of flowering plankton,
That plateau in the wind, in the spring, in the stars.

LYRIC

This spring is on your loom, Penelope;
Your fingers frozen and swift, your silver knife
In the threads of rain, in the rags of wind,
In my memory of a summer dress,
Of the movement opening it as light opens a flower –
Why do you unravel that pattern,

How will you repeat the design of spring, your allotted task,
Already disturbed by your game of patience?
The decision is not in your fingers,

And only the pattern on the loom falls victim.
You will repeat it clumsily and without love;
At dawn frost is on the peach blossom
Like salt on a wound,
                          and the air in the room
Blue with sleeplessness.

REPORT ON ICARUS

We assume he fell. The boy flew into the air, bright,
Up the blue vertebrae of wind, a muscled swimmer,
Open like a rose over the shrinking labyrinth –
Look, it is reduced to an equation, girdled by the dark blue of
    water
And the green silver of olives.
                        The air accepts the boy
Who drinks it, choking but certain, wiser
Than the birds he overtakes. We only assume he fell:
Horribly empty azure over some long-ago island,
A winged signal flash in the morning sun,
Quickly extinguished.

But there is no proof: ask the fish
Who allegedly ate those sun-bitten eyes,
Draw that tangent to the flank of the deepest ocean,
To the flesh of light, think now,

Imagine that smile behind the blue,
The moral about mimicking the young gods –

A smile behind the wind, an orbit of pure flame
Drawn in a field of yellow asphodels.

THE GUARD IN COLCHIS

The guard in Colchis is invisible;
You only hear his footstep, and the roll of shingle
In the ancient sleeplessness of foam on the rim of the sea.

Not a sail; in the morning wet winds
Tangle the stems of air, slowly growing wild,
Missing the familiar voices;
                                          in the evening, rain in the hills,
By night the green rattle of pebbles in the moonlight;

And after the act, after love, after poison,
After the renamed constellations,
After so many books opened in the wind
Like soiled magnolia flowers,

The guard on the shore, invisible, forgotten,
Stares at the open green sea,
For someone must stay, meaningless,
If the game is to be played correctly.

And the right password rusts in his mouth
Like a key in an unneeded keyhole.

ODYSSEUS AMONG THE PHAEACIANS

I know: I cannot go on until I remember
My justification; and that is tattooed on the shoulder of air,
Shouted into the flame, the spray, the ship's wake
Raked flat by the fingers of winds;

And so I am what I am: my origins obscure;
Plunged after a storm into a shore's flowery shingle,
I strove to unravel my eyelashes, sealed
With bitter crystals of salt;
                              but ready at once for anything,
I thirstily breathed the air filled with sparkling voices
Busy with their game, outside me;

Now I can speak, can try to explain
The coincidences: this tree which rises straight as altar smoke
From a distant sacrifice, this girl's eyes
Green as the sea before my first sailing,
This sun set in blue, like the clouded stone
In a ring I left with someone as a pledge of return;

Return? Here the breeze rustles the trees,
Flowers stretch upwards, wine glows in the cup,
And that woman's fingers feel familiar, the cool of snow
On my shoulder, firm as a pomegranate, cracked open with sun –

And yet, O king, give me a boat, give me a winged ship
That I may leave this certainty, so alien to its birth;
Listen, the sea is sounding:
                              so many voices
In that silvered blue, so many possibilities,
But one of them is true.

TO ELPENOR

Of course, there's always a shorter way,
Avoiding the winds, the currents, the years,
And all the disorientation of open sea
Between the tangled yarn of stars, avoiding the shores
With their dubious fires, the uncertainty of landfall,
And every new departure with a decimated crew.
But at what cost? Lost images shimmer
In the wind, and somewhere a crack
Eats away the smooth parapet waiting for you
To lean there, weary, one afternoon –
                                    but you did not come;
And in some cove the sea now senselessly whispers
The echo of your name, at the precise place, the precise time,
But no one calls you.
                        This, then, must be the penalty:
This pure absence which is your awareness,
Your emptiness printed into the summer air,
The cinders of a fire which did not burn.

OCEAN

Green and jet-black evergreen water, pregnant
With its act of blossoming, by a wind which
Shakes its salty stamens till spindrift fills the
Air of the mainland.

Salty thrushes' feathers and humid thunder,
Salty cries of herring gulls in the glow of
Summer, slanting wet down the current's scarp, the
Hem of the mainland.

All of this is shore, and this rock the place a
Continent remembers itself, right here where
It begins; the roar of a shallow sea, the
Ring of a bell-buoy.

Goat-track through the junipers, then a motor
Sounds a signal over the slate-black nab, an
Empty house, a weather-vane sniffs the miles, the
Years and the showers.

Images dissolve here, a whirl of sea-birds
Driven back inland on a gale; our speaking
Ages quickly, timeless, upon this no man's
Land of a shoreline.

Beautiful and perilous is this space, for
It remembers ringwise; the wind speaks tongues of
Earth and tongues of water, all indecisive,
Age-young and spray-wet;

See – the boat emerges beyond the point, a
Shift of no importance, a short-lived image
Is defeated; damp in the thrush's song, a
Stain in my hearing;

Features of unease, but behind them, balance:
Ancient python charmed by its own entwining,
Serpent flesh which teems with the silver grubs of
Thundery showers.

JOANNA FROM RAVENNA

1

A ship on the sea, a bird on the runway of wind,
Joanna between petals of gold
In the marshes, between rain, wind, sun,

Joanna, sister of the years and the towers
Heavy with wind, leaning into the mud;
Joanna, sister of the star returning

Over the gentle skin of melted snow,
Joanna, sister of the will-o'-the-wisp –

Joanna wrapped in the fish-scales of her gown,
With a smile smouldering among the gold
Amid the teeming of insects hard and shiny, buzzing
Green like the ring on her finger;
Her eyes are two immemorial midnight seas,
All their depth distilled into two droplets.

Joanna, a fixed star; and rain
Coming from the ocean to her window;
A star fettered with the tongue of death,
Joanna breathes, Joanna smiles.

2

A ship on the sea, lightning in the year,
A dam in the hills, the humming of a turbine;
Joanna, sister of time, glitters on.

These words remember her. This wind
Lashing the window with late winter snow
Last summer touched her eyes,
Lips and hand, and her emerald ring.
And now, as I write her name,
Joanna listens to the pen, glitters on.

Joanna between the petals of gold
With a smile smouldering like phosphor
Listens to the swell of the sea, the flash of a bird,
The turning of a turbine before the dam bursts,
And to these words which will touch her

With the fingers of my fire, after me.

WANDERER'S NIGHT SONG

Winter's constellations grow denser towards the south,
The sky obsessed with the ordered fantasies of fire,
Orion emerges sprawling from the sea,
And slowly climbs to his feet, wet Cyclops,
Unerring in the desperate steadiness of his slow
Motion, as he straddles his allotted angle
On an ancient matrix of flame.
       Upright
By midnight, a figure in praise of equilibrium,
Only to tilt his forehead deep towards the sea, precise
Even when forced to bow down to the water,
Then breathe the sea – the drowned undead returns.
So what is left
     to our daily lot?
The treacherous no man's land from after-image to measure,
The pattern of foaming roses upon the pebbles
At dawn, after the work of sea is done.

HOLY FOOL

The years of wrath are coming,
And drops of fire are singing,
Swept on by a leaden wind.

Time is losing its measure,
The sands of earthly deserts
Sift to the lower abyss.

The bird recalls the wave which
Gave its motion a birth, and
Form remembers the formless,

The tongue recalls the voices
Floating with pollen over
The line of a primal shore,

And ice recalls the flame which
Used to contain it, melded
With roses, an eye, with rains,

And lovers waken when they
Touch each other in sleep, with
Fingers of one memory,

For in them is distance and
The exact measure of ash,
Which will not intermingle;

Everything hums and babbles
Beneath this dome so solid,
Where echo meets with echo,

Within this ravaged hearing,
Within this fated forehead,
Within this overfilled flesh:

For my fate is to witness
The onset of this recall
Which brings things back to their source,

Like seas on heaven's highways,
Like a name when it dissolves
To swarms of innocent voices:

Swept on by a leaden wind,
The drops of fire are singing,
The years of wrath are coming.

ABRAHAM TO HIMSELF

Bitter is this sand upon the shore, my offspring,
A great nation weeps in my loins,
Cruel is this covenant, unjustified measure,
And long are the ways of the flesh;
                                        here a bush
Burns with fire, there the sea rolls open like a book
For me to write a sentence in an illegible script,
And fire writhes in the mouths of prophets,
And the dust will not settle upon the roads,
And a pestilent crop of stakes travels with the tents –
But capricious are the angels, capricious the law that draws them
Towards a decision, towards the long and terrible love
I am making with eternity;
                                    my seed cries out
And praises thee, for so it must, thou who spreadest my bed.

THE DARK PROVINCE

Murmurs crumble with the crunch of gravel
In the long tunnel,
                            cracked hooves clatter,
We hold on to each others' voices and shoulders
In the darkness of the final world;
                                            drops of light seep through,
A wick fed with the thin oil of memory, another,
We ride on beneath the roots, beneath the years,
We share our ration of bitter poppies with the hungry shadows,
Our faces frighten us, from afar, at the exit.

Somewhere here all paths cross
Before their final parting,
And the track of the beast is confused
With the track of the angel at the still, terrible centre:
He who stays will regret it,
He who goes will regret it.

OF THE BUILDERS

'manent opera interrupta, minaeque
murorum ingentes . . . '
                              But the masons leave
For the lime-pits of time, with flowers, chaff, ashes,
Their plans are spattered with blood, lost,
And the golden plumb-line of sun says: the world is leaning,
Bedded in a base where the fingers
Of ancient waters touch the foundation.
But feel the walls: the glow stays on your hands.

In that glow I see an impregnable city, raised
On a plateau I do not recognise;
                              the winds
Flutter down like peacocks, tame, in its gardens,
Star-roe hatches in fountains, there
Every movement of the chisel is repeated, guarded
In perfect stone, in a new order
Which is, perhaps, more perfect through misfortune.

IX

Dubrovnik,
A Winter's Tale

TRAVELLER BEFORE DUBROVNIK, JANUARY

The first thunder, intoxicating syllables of speech
Between the palate and the clumsy tongue
Of the young year,
                    still present in the fleshy silence
Of the midday sea,
The sun at the hinge of the compasses describing the town
With a line of fire, an arc of shadow;
A stone garland wreathed around
The smooth forehead of the centuries, without a wrinkle
Betraying an effort of memory,
                              and islands
At anchor, strong points of immobility,
Green in the slow silver of the ebbing tide –

So may I remember that picture
Exposed on the coastline of sight,
That town in a ring of towers, a ring
On an apple,
            the target of Zeno's arrow

THE SCRIBE

Three wicks on the oil-lamp, three petals
Of the primal rose, beaten into flame long ago
In the goldsmith's game of air,
                              quiver
Above the tide of letters which fills the page
With the smoke of voices,
                          with the after-images of deeds,
Where the adjective unites with the noun
In love and hatred of the embrace
Which will shine over the hand's ashes.

A drumming on the road. A cicada cries
With the voice of hot iron as it touches water,
And night moves slow in her armour of fire.

The servants of the letters die at dawn
When the page is full, the sky empty,
The ink running dry, the pen stranded –

With three petals of fire upon their dying breath.

VOICES – FINIS REIPUBLICAE

Let a herald set out for the coast, and the Dark Province;
Sea instead of seal-wax,
The sand of centuries on the scroll –

And yet, who is there to listen to that speech
Set in the dark gold of seven locks,
Saying yes and saying no
And whetting wisdom as the sea grinds the pebbles
With the terrible gentleness of the stubborn centuries?

The pomegranate is flowering, tiny plant-like flame
Inventing a fruit of embers,
Red food of the dead.
                    From the towers
Banners are singing, or are they swans?

_____

By the waters of the Adriatic we wept –
The sea swept us away from the moment
Where our shadows were left for ever,
Shortened in their midday of defeat.

ARGOSY

Through time without a pilot, under full sail,
Over seas never drunk dry,
Always the same direction, under the whirl of winds
Scattering the embers of heaven,
Galleons.

Compasses have unfolded into roses,
The charts show peace and the crimson of snows,
A dumb angle on the sextants,
We sail.

There is no shore this side of air,
Just a word like a fire in the night
Showing an imagined rock, a reef,
Perhaps a memory reduced to a signal;
Over a sea without a shore, in a wind without an anchorage,
Galleons.

Round the perfect circle of a sentence
Dissolving on lips of flesh,
With cargoes which still arrive
At intended destinations,
With the angels' wing-beat of gulls
In a wind wet with weeping,
In the meridian shadow of a black sun
We sail.

ONOFRIO

Clear, refracted water,
Mnemosyne's murmur in Illyrian stone,
Pigeon-down the colour of clouds on the south wind
In the dance of my droplets,
My dream distilled to a law;

I have seen their faces, the pock-marked cheeks
Of thirst's trumpeters:
A smile lives in them, like thunder
In the shiver of the laurel leaf;

Invisible gardens of air, colonised
After the rippling, after my will,
Burgeon blue, evergreen –

One winter I sailed away:
I return with the voice of thirst, laughing
In liquid syllables.

SAINT BLAISE

I am a saint entering a dream, a herald of arms
Waking the combs of fire on the ramparts
In a dawn frozen into tradition,

A doctor from Cappadocia, a martyr
Multiplied over every ocean on my chasuble,
Like so many golden ducats struck in a bitter mint
Between the double matrix of sky and sea –

My eyes have grown dim there on the walls
Where they wove love into my cloak of stone,
Within arm's length of the sea; the guardian of four small
    directions,
The password of the four winds; the taste of salt on stone
Sings my metamorphoses.

To oblivion my name tastes bitter,
To stories sweet.

THE MASONS

The measure is in the stone, and the tongue of earth is crushed
In the voices of the chisels, seeking each other
In the echo of dust, like children's voices
Between the raindrops;
$\qquad$ sometimes we recognised
A scream or a word, trapped it,
Set it upright in air. We found the measure of walls,
The weeping of crenellations, the smile and the vine,
The movement of a beast rising from the stone
Like a star from the sea: innocent, washed clean –

We measured the stone with a yard of iron,
With our imperfect love;
$\qquad$ we translated
An unknown tongue into known forms,
And celebrated that unspoken agreement
With the stronger measure of substance;

Then the earth shook –

Somewhere there had been a mistake,
$\qquad$ unclear even in the flash
Of dust settling, of the tongue melting
Into its genesis, like water;

When the blood was dry
We tried again.

THE RAMPARTS OF DUBROVNIK

I wrote to you about the walk,
$\qquad$ in ink
Of the sea's ashes, of the vision of others' eyes.
They were towers with strange names,
Tempered like iron in the forge of an age-old tongue:

A Winter's Tale   157

Asimon, Dead Bell, Kalarinja, Drezvenik –
Sounds pleasing to the wind, and to the gulls
Circling deep beneath the ramparts, with the flight
Of a shuttle on the green loom of sea;
They were steps between terraces of emptiness
Piled high with ozone, crenellations
Lopped languidly like flowers from a stem,
And the creak of a hinge as the wind changed direction.
I breathed that air clean of history
Evaporating slowly like rainwater
From a stone basin;
                    what remains is dross,
Broken pictures, jumbled letters, the bed of gods
Abandoned after love, the impression of bodies in the sand;
A blazing sword of sun hovered over the towers,
And time could not return
To the gardens of stone.
                    I climbed
Onto platforms wrenched from the defences
Over a sea playing with its own reflections
Like a child with a mirror; below the wall
A sea the colour of hyacinths and Saracen flags,
A sea murmuring sentences far distant
From the meaning of the moment which overhears them.
I was alone, as I told you,
In the shadow of invisible wings, crucified
Between the twin angels of wind and light –
Before a grinning destiny,
                    defenceless.

PORTAL: PIETÀ

You are slipping from my knees, century by century,
But we remain in that balance, imperfect
On the surface of a perfect grief, like oil
On water.
        Footsteps beneath us
And a door the colour of bile and tar,
Voices, words and years
In their unique similarity, from moment
to moment. So we are trapped
In a stone pivot of pain, suspended
Over the continuation of destiny, shackled
To the borderline of the love between stone and iron –

And beneath the merciful rains,
Beneath the gentle filth of pigeons,
We darken like the back of a mirror
Turned towards emptiness.

PUSTIJERNA

I walked through those streets, at every corner
Losing another chance
Of returning unchanged.
                    The angel of oblivion
Broke his wings following my footsteps
Along a trail of blind window-arches; there was the slap
Of wet linen in the wind, and a woman's voice
Twisted into song like iron into lace,
Full of choked fire.

Why was I looking for that garden,
A drop of green plasma, a vine-shaded terrace, an orange tree,
A garden which had migrated long after the word, after the scent,
Into a stone shell, the ruins of a long-lost speech?

I could hear the sea behind the wall; that was
The only password for return,
Eye to eye with the blazing pitch of images,
With the terrible wholeness of memory.

I return suddenly older,
As if after first making love,
As if from battle.

AHASUERUS IN DUBROVNIK

I entered by the Pilé Gate
Beside a guard of freezing clay;
The port was ablaze in the red of morning,
A brief rose fed with the smell of tar.

Water babbles from the well in the square, and the twins
On their stone tower, their bronze flesh dying green,
Peddle in honest measures the time pawned
By the fathers of the city fathers, without a ticket;

I'm trying to find the owner,

My task is deathly serious,
Weariness filtered from my blood
Is settling like gold in the cups of my joints;

I have worn away the metal leaves of door-knockers,
My steps have thinned a thousand stone stairs;
                                        they all
Led to a wall;
                behind the wall, the sea,
That classroom image of fate.

I left by the Ploče Gate
On the evening of the same day, unmentioned
In archive or ledger, in the history of the art –
Beautiful, as I remember – of disappearing.

HOMAGE TO DUBROVNIK

A tongue's ashes in a dead mouth
Are honey in a hollow tree
To the mouth of the chronicler,
History perishes without stones –

This was the song of the sea surrounding the city
In the south wind, a wind of winter fruits
Through lance-shaped leaves, a wind of foam
Beneath the foundations of towers;
                          but error creeps in
With the first stone syllable of the translation
From this speech into yours, O city,
Beauty without a dictionary,
Insubstantial substance.

Fistful of pure cinders,
A flame in a new mouth is raising you higher;
What is lost without measure
Returns as measure
And settles inside your name like honey inside the comb.

X

Of the Works of Love
or
Byzantium

LAMENT OF THE CHRONICLER

Our works are bounded by emptiness,
Their edges brittle, islands strewn across the sea;
How much silence on every feeble word,
How much sky on every standing column,
How much terrible harmony in the ruins!

And what is hope but a dream of wholeness,
A concord of shores, a scream forced legibly
Into a sentence, as a stone into an arch;
But our works bounded by emptiness
Are but a poor imitation of the stars' contagious fires;

Who may bind them with form? Derive a continuation
Out of us, out of our misfortune? What is the language
Of the sweet mouth on the far side of wisdom?
While in the spherical eye of an angel or beast
The images may be wedded differently –

Alas O city, sand-castle on the beach!
Hear the rise of the wave and the rustle of absurdity
Lacing its edge, as it passionlessly erases our marks;
Who may complete the manuscript, this book which emptiness
Flicks through with fingers of flame?

EVENING ON THE RAMPARTS

And the tears betraying a hope on our cheeks
Are dried by the wind of late afternoon
With the salt silver of the tide ebbing over the rocks –

The meadow of fire amid the sea is empty,
Its flowers gone to seed, its hives deserted,
A wild pomegranate is ripening,
                              red food of the dead,
On the long-shadowed slopes.

Look, a light is settling
On our heads, on our shoulders,
And flowing into our farewell kiss
Like the sea into the taste of sacramental wine –

Our weapons, dumb devices of love;
The sun lights the flames on our lances
And the beast's Cyclopean eye observes us
Through the gates as they creak open.

STYLITE

The easiest was the climb,
                              and before that
The decision down there in the dust, at the base
Of the pillar, perfect even without me.

So here I am in equilibrium –
Flying without wings, I circle an infinite point,
Neither heaven nor earth,
                              on top of the column
Where I began to doubt –

Look, my thighs are withering, and my ribs
Peer in curiosity through my skin; the flesh is eaten
By the poison of undigested time,
                              on top of the pillar
Where the wind rocks me, where I burn like a wick
Whose candle never changes;

Now I have only my words,
A blessing for the market, the hubbub beneath the column,
The scratching of mules, the clink of scales –

And the stars, scarcely any closer,
At night when the square is deserted, and my shadow
Unhappy on the pure shadow of the column:

You will know me by my ashes.

DE ADMINISTRANDO IMPERIO

This havoc of others' memories will be
History,
                    these words groping for one another
In the dark of the unsaid – the real, perhaps –
As it screams from oblivion;
                                    but stars
Have no history, only time
Expressed in the pure measure of fire
And inflicted without warning;
                                    hence I write
Of peoples rising from the wet clay
And waking, without memory, at the gates
Of my city; I write these letters
So the onset of their maturity, uncertain
Tonight, might somewhere be imagined . . .
Tiredness is closing my eyes: I rinse them
With suspect water from the clepsydra;
                                    I write,
And the sound of the birth of letters on white
Returns from the future, louder
In the echo, like the howl of the wind,
Like the crash of clashing armies.

BYZANTIUM II

A strategist over a map, and a lawgiver,
And golden sand in the hourglass;
                                    maturity
In the eyes of children, and wisdom in the game
Beneath the cypresses, where short flames of grass
Lick letters from the stone, letters which the air
Repeats from memory;
                            and cupolas in the heat
Of a midday heavy with repetition; the sea
At the foot of the city, and the frontier snows
Scribbled with footprints: those of wolves
Confused with those of strangers. A seal on a letter,

or Byzantium   167

And in the ring the motion of a dead hand.
Processions wind along the walls
In eternal celebration of an unbounded moment;
A bee buzzes age over the flower, a star
Drops its winged shadow like an anchor
Into the shallow sea. The battle goes on.

To endure loneliness, without the consolation
Of changing glory for innocence, without a break
In the solemn and weighty sentence.
A tongue, more and more incomprehensible, celebrates
The movement which gave it life, now far away
At the centre of a perfect, lost circle.
A wind over the marches; the long promontories
Of lances shed sparks into the sea of the afternoon.

A strategist over a map, a scribe over a document
Concerning an attempt at eternity. In the brambles
Burn the eyes of the basilisk; the hunter
Moves the mirror warily, ever-wearier
With concentration; tongue of snake
And crest of cock, and a final glance
Eye to eye, like a strange justice
At the end of a forced ordeal.

The sentinel at the gates of the city crosses himself
With a gesture which knows no consequences.
At night, chains lock the harbour
And a wick burns in the emperor's room.
And the Pantocrator in the gold of the apse,
In the greatness of perfect absence,
Repeats the gesture of pure blessing.

And may this night be longer than all other nights
And may its power last beyond the measure
Already lost in the reckoning of battle:

When maturity returns its glance to its image,
Dangerous without a mirror, without a ruse,
Like the first beast on its first morning.

OF THE WORKS OF LOVE

The works of love are scattered through the world
Like the scars of war;
                       but grass grows fast
Over the battlefield, and the wet ember of earth
Bursts into flame to restore the terrible virginity,
As before the embrace, before the remembering,
Before the voices at dawn, with lips just parting:
The works of love are in dispute –

And when the wall crumbles, and when the garden grows wild,
Love loses out;
                       but listen to the screams of the birds
Over the cove where the sea learns from lovers
A different tenderness: time is impartial,
And the world is love's task,
                       the long rehearsal
Of immature gods.

MEMORY OF AN ORCHARD

Don't forget that orchard, Melissa, the orchard
On the tumbling slope of a summer already old,
Like a word the instant you say it;
                       it had been picked
Bare: only a few late fruits ripened
Between the dark, flickering leaves, dry at the edges:
Fire had changed direction.
                       We spoke in a language
Like water: quick on the surface,
Sparkling and sweet to a thirsty memory.
                       It's strange
How fate unpacks the makings of our past, for us,
For future memory: now I remember your gesture,
Your hand outstretched for a random gift – an unthinking,
Irrevocable testament. Evening fell quickly:
The smoke of smouldering branches, the milky drop of a star;

As we left, you walked a step ahead of me
Through an orchard suddenly heavy with all the fruit of earth
Which no one picks,

                    whose taste is unknown.

'THEN YOU MAY HAVE SAID . . . '

Then you may have said:
                    'But still I think
The most beautiful thing is what we love
With intuition in our soul', unaware you were repeating yourself,
That you were a mirror of a sister's lips
Eaten away by the sea in some ancient apple-grove of spray;
I heard you merged with the voices of waves, with
The invisible silver which sings on cicadas' wings
In afternoon hordes;
                    or then you may have
Stayed silent: it's all the same. In a clear time
Everything is already uttered, the space separating
Word and deed, fire and rose, is repealed,
Misfortune excluded:
                    this is where I listen to you
Tonight, as September's gaudy flame consumes the summer
In the whispering woods, and the familiar stars depart
Once more, like armies, for their winter quarters.

THREE VERSES

And our love will justify us in the end;
If fire can bind the brittle stone of ages,
Decay, with ties of lime, fire will assemble
Letters into words,

Legible the chronicle, dreadful the seal,
But our love will justify us in the end –

                              X · *Of the Works of Love*

A perfect rose of ash will be imprinted
On the other side;

Your skin, Melissa, raises a splash of spray
Into the thirsty sky; I build you a shrine,
For our love will justify us in the end,
Set the measure straight.

BYZANTIUM III

Black and golden widow, Lady
Walled into the north of the tallest tower,
Listen: the air, spattered with swallows' cries,
Is singing to you here, in the last window;

In it is sea, and wisdom,
And a grain of flame from the fields
Where the plough, overpowered by lightning,
Has melted in the furrow,

And a bee from an untended hive, sister
To the snakeweed, bitter with her own honey,
Is humming on a long thread of late sun;

Your husbands in the sand, in the sky,
In goatskin, in the memory woken
By the blood on your perfect hands;

Your sons, man enough at last
For your loneliness, your bed,
Are losing their reason, with your name
On their incestuous lips, and bearing
Starry children in their flesh;

You, in the beauty of all you remember,
Empty-handed upon the tallest tower.

or Byzantium   171

WORD OF THE WARRIOR ON THE BATTLEMENTS

With no choice, no dice, no pretence,
In this world reduced and pure
(Gird it with voices – a cry
Flies round the towers faster than a bird),
In the ruins to come, in the brood
Of the years of wrath, of snakes which lick our ears
Already filled with the roar of the beyond,
Already filled with future,
                                    here
Where a defeated maturity unites us
On the parapet, on the crumbling wall,
We will settle our accounts before we go –
That the misdeed be deducted from the deed
And, when our blood is mixed with dust
To beget the same mud, that the same measure
Be credited to a passionate eternity;
At night, beside our weapons and the fire,
The hourglass empties;
                              our voices
Already fill the abyss above,
                                    and the smoke
Of the stake where our bones will burn
Sinks with the sand into the abyss below.

CISTERN

The voices of thirst are retreating
Into the walled-in depths:
                              fainter and fainter
Gleams the sky, further and further falls the stone
Prised from a empty parapet;
In the air a drumming, the sob of a bird,
The smell of foreign lands –

The sons of winter, when they come,
Will chew the bitter roots of water;

See yourself in my mirror,
Autumn's midday sun.

SONG OF THE STATUE IN THE EARTH

In another garden, my face,
Just invented, is slowly turning
Towards a preciser pattern of stars;

                                        here, I no longer
Have a face: the back of my head smiles
At the wrath of earth, the labour of darkness
In my lobeless ear;

                  the wind
Which blows from the future does not move
The roots which envelop me, the heavy wings
Of an angel earthed to the moment
Of a higher light's duration;

                           O leaves,
Thousand eyelids in motion!
And the roots slip away from me
And a drop of rain trickles down my shoulder
Which an unknown hand is already touching
In another garden.

AUTUMN

The hawk in the clear void homes in
On the threat's very centre, soaring
Along the locus of light and wind
Plotted beneath the arc of its wings;

                            resistance
Wheels to intercept the bird, goading its eye
To a swift scan of stubble and woodland,

or Byzantium

Bristling its feathers; an invisible keep
Thrusts archers onto its ramparts;
                                                leaves
Tremble in the blue air, and redden;
The colour of wine-lees, of a horse
Returning from battle, empty-saddled,
Head bowed, its nostrils flecked with foam.

BYZANTIUM IV

My God, I do not understand this summer –
Your glory evades me in the roar
Of feuding voices in the noonday darkness;
Fragile gold glimmers on the edge
Of the leaf: the air is full of traitors,
To what measure was all this created –

For I cannot see the wave, I only see the ship
In an inverted nadir, its motion
Nailed like an open hand,
All its oars raised, rigid and dripping;
This summer is rainy, the trees black,
The book spattered, the letters smudged –

My God, the words You spoke were simpler then,
When You drew a wet shroud of clay
Over the face of earth, with a motion
Where misfortune reached its fullness,
Reconciled with the beginning and with the end,
Like honey in a hive after the swarm is dead –

Now the dust of Your wall, crumbling
In the rain, is growing small, ugly wings,
A mob of numbers and words mills around us –

Before the gates of snow stands a hard summer,
Great wet trees, Your mumbling
Revealing no certain word, no certain number.

THE MASONS OF BABEL

Did we, what did we sing on the scaffolding
Of the tower, most of it still in memory?
What fire was on our tongues, happy
A hundred times on its own hearth, bright
With the stone's rising, the groan of the windlass,
Did we, what did we sing on the scaffolding,

When the tower was a measure beyond all
Possible misfortune, and the risen stone
The measure's measure, and the trowel
Love's weapon in the excited air –
Did we, what did we sing as the herald frowned,
His hand raised to let the babel begin,

The abandoned windlass ran amuck,
The stone thundered down the tower, as
Lightning's signature set fire to the plans,
And we stared at each other in blankness, with eyes
Transformed in fear to those of forest beasts,
And scattered, flinging down our trowels,

Then what did we sing, what did we forget
As we quickly learnt the cause of a future
Of misfortune? Time will dismantle our tower
At leisure, stone by stone, as we teach babies
To babble in a tongue heavy with our ashes,
With the taste of sinful embers.

JACOB'S STONE

for A. Č.

Oh lucky man who knows his pillow when he wakes,
A purposeful rock in the wilderness, the
Cornerstone of a vertical dream, and says, trembling:
It's dreadful, this place –

He sets the stone erect in a memory greater than
The desert, and buries the bounds in a meadow
Of blood, between the flowers and the pollen
Borne on a black wind blustering from the future;

For the lips of dawn are tight, the dew is poisoned,
Drops of night sky scattered on the bed
Of a tangled love; only the stone remains

And the fiery reek of oil in the morning,
The sacrifice, the random price of hope
Forced to burst from a stone, a wild vine

For the drunkenness of sons who will forget
The art of a terrible dreaming.

ORPHEUS ON THE RAMPARTS

This is the line where song fears to tread,
This is a wind which spits on the lamp,
Rolls back the bird in flight, breaks bones,
This is my echo torn to shreds, these are my syllables
Blinded by the touch of the were-air of exile –
It is time for another death;

They will rip out my tongue, swollen
With bitter buds, wrench my arm with its lyre
From my shoulder,
                              too late –
I am already on the other side,
Already in my homeland, where the roots unravel,
Already rising to my feet, recognising the tunnel:

Circular, terrible, perfect orbit –
This is the time for song.

DARK HERACLITUS

Fire flares to a measure, fire dies to a measure:
Here I also have my genesis,
Measure translated into task,
The move of a flame in a mirror –
                              which is
Formed of darkness and silver, of snow
Which falls like flakes of lightning, frozen
Resistance to the gouging of the flash –
Now I am here,
With a few words to justify myself
In the feverish instant I am
Marked with my name;
                      night has
Combed the black fire of the cypress
With a diamantine wind, and stars are trembling
In place of other stars
To flare to a measure, to die to a measure.

BYZANTIUM V

Memory's lucid voices, clear droplets,
Like the works of wind, cloud and sea:
Water in the veins of the cypress,
Fickle pearl on a vertical string –
The word's ancient chance to create
Its precise fate, maybe a song:
So we listened, last night, to a shower of rain
In a garden where the aloe, the myrtle grows,
Where rosemary, sage, and basil –
Sparks which sing, wet gold
On the walls, already worn thin, of a church
Gloriously chiselled out of the summer air;
We remembered. But what was the song?
Look, morning's cantankerous voices
Are rising from the upper ocean:
                              a cold

Shadow falls across the sundial,
The wild vine, the lead roof,
The coastal plain; look, beneath the pines
Black horses are lifting their heads
To sniff the flame in their manes –
What memory is slipping her wedding ring upon the finger
Of the youngest of us, as the pen covers the virgin page
With the words *misfortune, misfortune, misfortune* –
The future: a huge tree,
And space this morning an empty training ground
For its forked shadow;
                              we are cold,
In the landslip of air a distant feathering of frost
And leaves dark with a familiar blood.

HOMELAND

Wandering in alien lands and cities,
Indecisive amid the images linking fidelity
To a beloved space, justified through memory,
My forehead against the stone of some fountain,
Or between hills crowned in beauty, where the clouds
Give birth to a young fire in an old bed,

My feet in some cold sea,
Where the edge of earth is rougher and voices raw,
Or in groves of olives, cupolas, towers –
In alien lands and cities, staring at a horizon
Where the sky divorces the land
With the bottomless sheen of Cyclopean gold,

My heart tight as the neck of an hourglass
I have composed a homeland,
                              piece by piece,
Of the signs which overtake me like justice
From the other side, where love needs no excuse
And love is our daily bread; and so I always return
In a circle girded with familiar names, like towers –

That is my homeland, my only certainty,
And the death I have gained the right to share:
All else is only a growth of picturesque ruins
Where a passer-by signs his name with a poem.

THE SEA DESCRIBED FROM MEMORY

Space, hollowed by rain's lost needles
And clear between the pines: a blue move of silver,
With every possibility assembled like an army
For the brief festival of an image;
                                    but up on the scarp
Children's voices fill the air with time, and water
Hisses between the rocks, wave repeats wave,
The keel ploughs the shingle of the cove;
There is no whole: it is terribly far to the centre
Of this tranquil power, its edges overgrown with lace –
Only a kinship of images, remembered deep in the soul,
Still sings a service to its source:
The dry snow of olive-groves, the moon in a quarry,
A pomegranate, crimson inside like the earth,
A pool of ink from the chronicle of the stars –

So that later, in some winter's room,
A beast, silver and blue, may rise
In the ear's draughty labyrinth: the sea.

RAŠKA

The stars over Raška are unlike other stars:
Their fuse short, their powder damp, the flash indistinct,
The Great Wain bogged down in blood and mud,
And the vampire hills crimson at dawn –

So why does an angel consent to stop
On the wall of a new church, to light up this space
Stamped with an unreliable splendour?

But he is sure to be a clear signal, hoist
In the midst of this uproar, where the weapons of love
Are forged in darkness, like posterity;

Summer and spring did the Lord create,
Thus sang the psalmist:
At peace are those who are destined
To be the middlemen of time –
                                        but
Love's fevered portion, the bronze weight of the heart,
Grows in the brief scale of maturity:
And so an angel holds court here.

CATENA MUNDI

Thracian hills, Illyrian mountains,
I love your names worn smooth by time
As rough pebbles are polished by streams;
                                        I remember
Your heavenly frontiers, disputed in the haze,
Green and white after the rain;
                                        I travel
Along river valleys where the voice of the storm recites
The alphabet of nations on the move, and the leaves
Are like flame, and the cries of the birds, high overhead,
Reopen the old scars of air;
Perhaps I should have stopped here –

But to me you seem more beautiful from the other side,
More beautiful on old maps which go yellow
At the onset of autumn;
                              pillars of heaven, hills
Invisible to an eye without love,
I drink light and water from the palm of my hand, at the foot
Of an unproven peak; the dead tranquilly observe me
From beneath the roots, beneath the stones.

BYZANTIUM VI

To dream, in some moment of forgetting, a new city
To the very last rampart – is this the reward
Awaiting the witnesses?
Cold is each stone
Upon the roads, cold each star
Over the cypresses, and cruel the images
Upon the wave of tomorrow's sea:
Roofs leprous with alien fire,
A breach in the wall, corpses in the streets
– In the gardens spring at its peak –
And a red-shod youth, overtaken by misfortune, his features
Indistinguishable since the work of steel, waits
With the rest for the quicklime, maybe the stake,
Or the curs' teeth –
And all this, Wisdom, under your very eyes.
Is this really the witnesses' prize: absence
From their testimony's aftermath? The scattering
Of the rose of their voices, their touches?
For they know full well that here
All is cut to the measure of misfortune;
                                            but
What is misfortune meant to measure?
Memory, perhaps, or forgetting
In an uncertain heaven, where they
Dare to dream a brand-new city
To the very last ramparts of jasper?

INSCRIPTION ON A FOUNTAIN

Here the mouth of shadow is deeper; and there
The time of thirst gathers more deeply, so where
The water fills the bowl till it overflows,
The measure of an infinite column grows –

If you're thirsty, bend your head to the streaming;
And cup your hand beneath the bubbles' teeming,
The babble of breeding drops, and drink: and blend
Your thirst into a moment which has no end.

IN THE PRESENCE OF THE DEAD

Cypress, chiselled stone and snake:
Three ways to be in the presence of the dead
At midday, when the icon-lamps are lit
In the salt orchards of the sea;

In the black tree's truncated shadow
Lives a time of continuation; letters
Link the stone with memory, resistance
To the nether silence, the home of the snake –

In the snake is slowed lightning: herald
Drunk on both worlds' milk, his forked tongue
Sings the twoness of the budding moment;

The triangular shadow of a star, out of position
In a field of words,
                          stains the silver
Of midday's ancient mirror.

TRAVELLERS IN WINTER

On our return we saw fires in the snow,
Brown bloodstains on the bandage of a midnight just healed
At the foot of the hills;
                and up there, on the slopes,
The unforgotten foam of last year's sea was returning
In the sign of a new innocence.
                    There was
The lightning flight of an angel through a crack
In the low sky, and our footprints, a murmur,
But not one star;
              then we understood: this was the nadir,
Frozen mud, the bottom of the well,
Where our footfall was mingled with despair
And the smoke of voices –
Then the rattle of a chain on the windlass above us,
Maybe just the wind coming down from the hills,
Feeling its way, blind as Oedipus –
And waiting, the final form of hope.

WRITTEN IN THE SILVER OF THE SEA

But at times we were so terribly close
To our homeland,
                              just the other side
Of the thinning air; we could overhear
Words fast and winged, a meaning sensed
In the clumsy translation of lightning;
We would flee in fright into the illusion
Of time, into a false equilibrium –
Everything essential we remember is an image
Before waking: chestnut and wild fig, reluctant
Flame in the ruins,
                              and all we call memory
Shines from the point of a long gleaming needle
Where the taste of fire mixes with silence
In the air over the ephemeral silver
Of a sea between two storms.

BYZANTIUM VII

Under the wise escort of our ghosts someone will walk, perhaps,
One day, along the contour of these battlements, where
We watched the sun, a copper weight tilting into the scale of night;
The sea will leach silver and flotsam onto the pebbles
Rounded with future gentleness; the air will be blue
With the smoke of our names;
                          but who will understand us?
For the centre will have shifted, the images will be changed,
Perhaps now joined to the stem: perhaps a flower –
And the works of love will merge into a speech, a tongue;
And then who would wish to compose our testimony
From these scattered syllables, from the cries
Caught by chance in some antique mirror,
In the surge of a wave? And why?
Will there be room tomorrow for this babel
In the serene memory of some angel, in the smooth memory
Of young waters? The memory of lovers?
Will anybody need the betrayed images
Of our love, and the sentinels out in the desert
With sand in their lungs, that meagre tongue of misfortune,
A quick punishment for maturity, an assigned defeat?
Or will the balance be more exact without us,
And the tongue of lovers sweeter without our voices
Mingled with death as the wind with flame,
As the source with the sea?

TRANSLATOR'S NOTES

How Orpheus Sang   (page 30)

11-syllable lines.

Ophelia   (p. 32)

11-syllable lines in the original, changed to non-syllabic tetrameter (4-beat line) in translation.

Wind   (p. 33)

Line 2: 'the hair on Hammer Peak's head': *maljama na grudima Maljena* – an irreproducible pun in the original, literally 'the hairs on the chest of the Hammer'.

Prayer   (p. 34)

In the original, 11-syllable lines throughout.

Requiem for a Mother   (p. 34)

In the poem 'My Mother's Memorial', from *The Passionate Measure*, we learn that Lalić's mother died in 1946, when he was 15. The epigraph is from Hölderlin's 'Menon's Lament for Diotima', part 3: 'Light of love! do you shine on the dead too, O golden one!'

This Great Big Moon   (p. 37)

'I wrote this on military service, after a night on guard duty.'

Rider   (p. 37)

11-syllable lines.

Wick   (p. 43)

11-syllable lines.

Fresco   (p. 47)

'A combination of two frescoes: one is the famous white angel from Mileševa, and the other exists only in my mind.'

Byzantium   (p. 48)

After the Western Roman Empire fell to the barbarians in the fifth century, the Eastern half of the Empire, with her capital Byzantium, survived for another thousand years. Even during the years of her decline, she exerted an enormous cultural, religious and political influence on the emerging Slav nations to the North and West.

Byzantium fell twice. In 1204 the leaders of the Fourth Crusade, on their way to the Holy Land, were persuaded by Venice to sack Byzantium instead (Byzantium was her main trading rival): anyway, the prospect of loot was more appealing than fighting the Saracens.

Though the Byzantine Greeks managed to wrest back control of their territories by mid-century, their Empire had been fatally weakened. During the fourteenth century, they proved unable to resist the gradual advance of the Ottoman Turks. Long stripped of territory, the city was finally taken by the Turks on May 29th, 1453.

The rhymed verses are syllabic, but with slightly different line-lengths and rhyme-patterns between the original and the translation.

Smederevo (p. 50)

In 1389 the Christian powers of the Balkans, in rare alliance, were crushingly defeated by the Ottoman Turks at the Battle of Kosovo, the Blackbirds' Field. The Turks, who already held all of the Byzantine Empire but Constantinople and its hinterland, looked set to add the Balkans to their possessions, though first they needed to take the Imperial City itself.

Their plans were struck a near-fatal blow by the invasion of the Mongol Emperor Timur (Tamburlaine) in 1402, when they lost the whole of their Asia Minor possessions. Using European Turkey as a power-base, the Sultans saw as their first aim the recapture of the rich Asia Minor provinces. In exchange for oaths of fealty, the Balkans were left more or less to their own devices, though they never united again against their overlords. Their respite was a long one, but once the reinvigorated Turks under Sultan Mahmoud II had taken Constantinople in 1453, the end was inevitable and swift.

Nevertheless, the last stronghold of the medieval Serbian state, the fortress of Smederevo – built by Despot Djordje Branković (who ruled from 1427 to 1456) – held out for another six years, until 1459. The largest castle in Europe, it is awesome even today. What it lacks in natural defences – it lies in the flatlands beside the Danube – it makes up for by the sheer size of its towers and length of its walls.

I have translated *Despot*, the highest rank of Byzantine nobility, as 'Prince'. This is in order to avoid any connotations of 'tyrant', which it does not have in the original.

Letter from the Knight Sinadin (p. 51)

When the Mongol armies swept into Asia Minor in 1402, troops levied from the Balkan vassal states fought alongside the Turks against the new invaders. In the fateful Battle of Angora (present-day Ankara), a heroic last stand by his Serbian knights failed to save Sultan Bayazit from a humiliating defeat at the hands of Timur the Great.

Death with a Falcon   (p. 52)

The 'Prince' is Serbian Despot Stefan Lazarević, who ruled from 1389 to 1427. He was the son of Despot Lazar, who fell in the Battle of Kosovo.

The Danube by Smederevo   (p. 53)

Pison is mentioned in the Bible as one of the world's four great rivers, which have their source in the garden of Eden. It is almost certainly the Danube. Donji Milanovac, the next town downstream, features in a poem from *The Passionate Measure*: 'Elegy, or The Danube at Donji Milanovac'.

Resava   (p. 54)

Resava, or Manasija, is one of Serbia's medieval monasteries, the finest of which were constructed during her last, illusory period of independence. Built for uncertain times, Resava is situated on the side of a steep valley and strongly fortified. It is famous not only for its architecture, but also for its frescoes: 'this poem is a translation of the frescoes.'

1804   (p. 55)

The First Uprising of the Serbs against a weakening Ottoman Empire took place from 1804–1812, under the charismatic Serbian leader Karadjordje.

Its crushing persuaded the wily leader of the more successful Second Uprising (1815–1817), Milos Obrenović, that negotiation and a step-by-step approach to autonomy were more likely to succeed. When Karadjordje finally returned to the new principality of Serbia, Obrenović had him murdered, sparking off a long enmity between their two dynasties.

The stake is for impalement (a favourite Ottoman method of execution), not for burning.

Princip on the Battlefield   (p. 56)

Gavrilo Princip's assassination of the Archduke Ferdinand and his wife, the act which sparked off the First World War, took place in Sarajevo on June 28th, 1914 – the anniversary of the Battle of Kosovo.

Perhaps the finest poem from the Kosovo cycle – 'Kosovska devojka' – tells of how a girl has been given three items by three brothers, one of whom she is to wed: a coat of many colours, a wedding ring, and a golden shawl. In the poem she searches the battlefield after the slaughter, only to hear that all three have died:

> Were I to touch a green pine tree,
> Even that green pine would wither.

Princip's imagined words reflect the folk-epic lines:

> All was blessed and just
> And pleasing to the dear Lord God.

Requiem (p. 57)

The massacre of Orthodox Serbs in the church at Glina (July 1941) was one of the most hideous acts of the Ustaša, the paramilitary force of the Croatian fascists during the Second World War.

After the German invasion in 1941, Hitler carved Yugoslavia up between Germany, Italy, Bulgaria, Hungary and the Nazi puppet state of Croatia, and proceeded to govern by divide-and-rule tactics. Tito's partisans represented a welcome force for unity in the face of vicious inter-ethnic and inter-religious bloodletting, and this played no small part in their success. It also meant, however, that this bloodletting was best not talked of publicly in post-war Yugoslavia – and certainly not in 1953, when this poem was written.

Chamber Poem for a City (p. 59)

Belgrade is built on a headland formed by the confluence of the Sava and the Danube; the Kalemegdan fortress occupies the bluff directly above the meeting of the two rivers. The city has been destroyed many times, most recently by Hitler's Luftwaffe, but has always risen again.

'Belgrade, white swan': Belgrade means 'white city'. It is a double quote – from the folk poems, and from the nineteenth-century Romantic poet Branko Radičević.

Melissa (p. 63)

'The name of a righteous woman who lived on the Isthmus. Demeter initiated her into her mysteries, about which she was sworn to secrecy. When the other women could not coax the secret out of her, they tore her to pieces. As a punishment, Demeter sent a plague to that region, but she transformed Melissa's remains into a swarm of bees.' *Melissa* still means 'bee' in Greek.

The original verse structure can best be described as free-form sonnet: rhymed, but not in a fixed scheme; with a largely hexameter rhythm, but without a fixed syllable-count. Most of the translations, however, are in pentameter rhythm.

A Perfect Autumn (p. 94)

11-syllable line.

The Sea After Rain (p. 99)

Sapphic verse-structure (see Introduction).

Algol   (p. 109)

I first met Ivan V. Lalić in 1978, when I was studying in Yugoslavia. On hearing that I was interested in astrology, he gave me a book from his father's collection: Johannes Fehlow's *Lehrkursus der wissenschaftlichen Geburtsastrologie* (Course in Scientific Natal Astrology), published in Thüringen, Germany, in 1934. It has this to say about the star Algol:

'Algol: ß Persei.   25° 3'.

From the Arabic *al-ghoul*, the demon. A dark companion circles the main star once every 69 hours, cutting off its light for 9 hours at a time. The ancient Chinese observed the change in light and said: full brightness means there will be dead as the sands of the sea, especially when Mars is near ... The Babylonians called it "the Boomerang" – or, as we would say nowadays, the guillotine of the heavens, for near the Sun it gives the risk of beheading. A famous example: Robespierre, who caused the violent death of many people, only to end up on the scaffold himself ...

It must be pointed out, however, that the star also has higher spiritual influences, to which only the most highly-endowed of individuals are receptive. This is perhaps the case with Mussolini ... '

The underlying theme of Lalić's cycle is the fear of nuclear holocaust.

Spring Liturgy for a Dead Poet   (p. 114)

Branko Miljković was one of the leading poets of the Yugoslav post-war period. His poetry was obsessed with death as the final, incommunicable experience, where the poem is the sole survivor. He hanged himself in 1961, at the age of 27.

The first part of Lalić's liturgy is written in 11-syllable lines, whereas part 3 is in blank verse. Parts 2 and 4 were not included in the 1969 collection, and are therefore not reproduced here.

The Singer and the King   (p. 116)

David and Saul.

Orpheus' Second Descent   (p. 119)

11-syllable line.

Nereid   (p. 121)

'Even today I enjoy that game in which an inlet (on Red Island, near Rovinj) changes into a woman, and back again.'

In Ancient Greece the Nereids were sea-nymphs, daughters of Thetis.

Kalemegdan   (p. 127)

See note to 'Chamber Poem for a City'.

A Bitter Summer's Fires Still Wheel   (p. 137)

This poem has the 4-beat, 8-syllable rhythm of the 'Dies Irae' (line 21 being a direct quotation). In 'Imago ignota' (*The Passionate Measure*) Lalić quotes, in turn, several lines from his earlier poem:

> What I see is the dream of geometry:
> Disintegration, defeat of the straight line,
> The grating melted around the hearth ...

In the translations, the quotations do not quite tally. This is because, when I came to translate the earlier poem, the demands of rhythm and metre meant that I could not keep the forms already published in the later poem.

Odysseus Among the Phaeacians   (p. 142)

After leaving Calypso's isle, Odysseus is shipwrecked on the coast of Phaeacia, where he wakes to the sounds of the Princess Nausicaa and her maidens playing ball by the shore while their washing dries in the sun. Received warmly by King Alcinous, it is here that Odysseus tells of his adventures, and asks for a ship to take him home. Though willing to let Odysseus stay and give him the hand of Nausicaa in marriage, Alcinous grants his request.

To Elpenor   (p. 143)

Elpenor was Odysseus' helmsman. The last night in Circe's palace, he had been sleeping on the roof, drunk after the evening's feasting, and missed the ladder when trying to descend again. In his hurry to go to Hades to ask the shade of the seer Tiresias about his destiny, Odysseus leaves him behind, unburied. When he eventually reaches the mouth of Hades, the shade of Elpenor is the first to come up to him, begging that his soul be put at rest and the anger of the gods be averted by giving him the proper burial rites.

Ocean   (p. 143)

Sapphic verse-form: see Introduction.

Joanna from Ravenna   (p. 144)

In the mosaic of Theodora and her court in San Vitale, Ravenna, Joanna stands two places to the Empress' left. The daughter of the commander Belisarius, she was renowned as one of the most beautiful women of her time.

192

Holy Fool   (p. 146)

8-syllable line in the original, translated as a 7-syllable line.

The Dark Province   (p. 148)

A Serbian folk-tale tells: 'A King was riding through the Dark Province, when he heard a voice say: "If you stop to pick us up, you'll regret it, if you pass us by, you'll regret it." He looked around but could see nothing but the pebbles under his feet. Puzzled, he picked up a pebble and put it into his pocket. When he regained the world of the living, he found that the pebble had turned into a diamond.'

Of the Builders   (p. 149)

'The work remains broken off, and the mighty / crenellations of the walls . . . ' – Virgil, *Aeneid* IV.88.

Voices – Finis Reipublicae   (p. 154)

Dubrovnik survived as an independent city-state on the Adriatic until 1792, when it was handed over without a fight to Napoleon's troops.

Argosy   (p. 155)

The English title, meaning a trading fleet, derives from Ragusa – the Italian name for Dubrovnik.

Onofrio   (p. 155)

Onofrio's fountain (named after its builder, Onofrio de la Cava from Naples) stands under a stone canopy at the foot of the Clock Tower. It was damaged by Serbian shells during the 1991 siege.

Saint Blaise   (p. 156)

The patron saint of Dubrovnik, whose figure appears in niches around the city walls and who was shown on the city's coinage.

The Masons   (p. 157)

Much of the city was destroyed in the catastrophic earthquake of 1667.

Portal: Pietà   (p. 159)

This is over the doorway of the Church of the Franciscan Monastery – another building badly damaged in the 1991 siege.

Pustijerna   (p. 160)

Pustijerna – the waste – was the part of the city most damaged by the 1667 earthquake. Traces of the destruction can still be seen.

Ahasuerus in Dubrovnik (p. 161)

Ahasuerus is the Wandering Jew of medieval myth. In the most usual version of the story, he was a cobbler who refused to let Christ rest at his door on His way to Calvary, saying 'Get off! Away with you, away!', at which Christ replied: 'I am going, but thou shalt tarry till I come again.'

De Administrando Imperio (p. 167)

This was a handbook on government written by the Emperor Constantine VII Porphyrogenitus for his son Romanus around the year 950. One of the things it speaks of is the coming of the Slavs to the Balkans.

'Then you may have said . . . ' (p. 170)

'But still I think . . .': the quotation is from Sappho.

Three Verses (p. 170)

Each verse has three 11-syllable lines, followed by one 5-syllable line.

Raška (p. 180)

In the mid-fourteenth century the Serbian Empire, under its leader Stefan Dušan, covered most of the Southern and Western Balkans, and seemed set to take over Byzantium itself. On Stefan's death in 1355, however, the Empire disintegrated into a number of 'despoties' (feudal principalities). The Despoty of Raška (Rascia) covered the territory of present-day Serbia South of the Danube. Its leader Lazar (ruled 1367–1389) attempted to unite the squabbling Balkan statelets to stem the Turkish tide: an attempt which met its end on the Field of Kosovo.

Catena Mundi (p. 180)

Old maps show an unbroken chain of mountains across the Balkans from the Black Sea to the Adriatic. This is not true: there is a gap, the Plain of Kosovo, where peoples and armies have passed – and clashed – for millennia. The most recent major battle at this strategic point was in the First World War.

Byzantium VI (p. 181)

Byzantium's last Emperor, Constantine XI, died defending the Gate of St Romanus against the final Turkish onslaught.
Cf. the New Jerusalem: *Revelations* XXI.

Inscription on a Fountain (p. 182)

11-syllable lines.

INDEX OF TITLES

Also translated by Francis R. Jones

IVAN V. LALIĆ
The Passionate Measure

This book is a complete version of *Strasna mera*, which received Yugo-slavia's major literary award in 1984. These strongly lyrical poems are ablaze with metaphors that since the disintegration of Yugoslavia have acquired an incidental and poignant resonance.

'Here in a translation fit to enter English verse [Lalić's poems] appear as they really are: intelligent, compassionate, composed. They are intact, they hold together, they quicken the mind and the heart in a most hopeful way.' – David Constantine in *Poetry Review*

'Rarely has poetry of the late 20th century been immersed in the inner world of the "metaphysical" with such incantatory power and reso-nance. Poem after poem ignites in a virtuoso display of metaphor and image.' – Gerard Smith in *The Irish Times*

'[Lalić's] lyrical and insistent work has been brilliantly translated from the Serbo-Croat by Francis Jones.' – Jill Waters in *The Independent*

HANS FAVEREY
Against the Forgetting

Francis Jones's translations capture both the musicality and the sinuous density of Faverey's Dutch in this extensive selection which introduces an important poet. His rich and thoughtful poetry developed from the fragmented, mysterious images of his early work to the more explicit and representational style with which he gained wider recognition.

Hans Faverey (1933–1990) was born in Dutch Guiana but grew up in Amsterdam. He was a clinical psychologist at the University of Leiden. He received the 1990 Constantijn Huygens Prize for his work as a whole.

Edwin Morgan writes in the Poetry Book Society's *Bulletin*: 'Hans Faverey ... made his reputation only gradually, as readers came to realize that his pared-down, quietist, totally unflashy poems were in fact both moving and thought-provoking ... He is a poet of losses and silences, of meditations on change and how change either undermines or strengthens our sense of reality.'

Some Poetry in Translation from Anvil

BEI DAO
Forms of Distance
Translated by David Hinton

ANA BLANDIANA
The Hour of Sand
Translated by Peter Jay & Anca Cristofovici

PAUL CELAN
Poems
Translated by Michael Hamburger

DICK DAVIS
Borrowed Ware
MEDIEVAL PERSIAN EPIGRAMS

LUIS DE GÓNGORA
Selected Shorter Poems
Translated by Michael Smith

FRIEDRICH HÖLDERLIN
Poems and Fragments
Translated by Michael Hamburger

GÉRARD DE NERVAL
The Chimeras
Translated by Peter Jay
with an essay by Richard Holmes

PABLO NERUDA
The Captain's Verses
Translated by Brian Cole

VASKO POPA
Collected Poems
Translated by Anne Pennington
Revised and expanded by Francis R Jones

ARTHUR RIMBAUD
A Season in Hell and Other Poems
Translated by Norman Cameron

GEORGE SEFERIS
Complete Poems
Translated by Edmund Keeley and Philip Sherrard

New and Recent Poetry from Anvil

HEATHER BUCK
Psyche Unbound

CAROL ANN DUFFY (ed.)
Anvil New Poets 2

HARRY GUEST
Coming to Terms

MICHAEL HAMBURGER
Collected Poems 1941–1994

JAMES HARPUR
A Vision of Comets

ANTHONY HOWELL
First Time in Japan

MARIUS KOCIEJOWSKI
Doctor Honoris Causa

PETER LEVI
The Rags of Time

CHARLES MADGE
Of Love, Time and Places
SELECTED POEMS

E. A. MARKHAM
Misapprehensions

DENNIS O'DRISCOLL
Long Story Short

PHILIP SHERRARD
In the Sign of the Rainbow
SELECTED POEMS 1940–1989

RUTH SILCOCK
A Wonderful View of the Sea

SUE STEWART
Inventing the Fishes

A catalogue of our publications is available on request